# How To Reverse Recession And Remove Poverty In

# INDIA

**Prove Me Wrong & Win 10 million Dollar**

## CHALLENGE WITHIN 60 Days

DR. NIAZ AHMED KHAN FRCS, PHD

*AuthorHouse™ UK*
*1663 Liberty Drive*
*Bloomington, IN 47403 USA*
*www.authorhouse.co.uk*
*Phone: 0800.197.4150*

*© 2014 Dr. Niaz Ahmed Khan FRCS, PhD. All rights reserved.*

*No part of this book may be reproduced, stored in a retrieval system, or transmitted by any means without the written permission of the author.*

*Published by AuthorHouse   12/10/2014*

*ISBN: 978-1-4969-9681-7 (sc)*
*ISBN: 978-1-4969-9682-4 (e)*

*Any people depicted in stock imagery provided by Thinkstock are models, and such images are being used for illustrative purposes only.*
*Certain stock imagery © Thinkstock.*

*This book is printed on acid-free paper.*

*Because of the dynamic nature of the Internet, any web addresses or links contained in this book may have changed since publication and may no longer be valid. The views expressed in this work are solely those of the author and do not necessarily reflect the views of the publisher, and the publisher hereby disclaims any responsibility for them.*

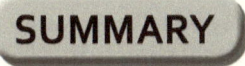

# SUMMARY

**MBCS applied on India**

**A Method to Address Economic Recession, Remove Poverty, Terrorism, Improve Law and Order, Reduce Drug Abuse, Inflation And Taxes in an Interest Free Based Economy.**

By: Dr. Niaz Ahmed Khan, FRCS, PhD

**ABSTRACT:**

I have developed a new financial instrument which will be much more valuable than the bonds or the treasury bills government sells in the open market to raise much needed funds to run the country. These are all interest based instruments and can only be used by institutions. The instrument I am proposing is without interest and will be used by everybody to purchase goods and services in the government and private sector resulting in up to 66% discounts. This is why these will be massively bought up front in large amounts in the shortest period of time of one month to run the country for at least a year and much more by the end of the year.

**INTRODUCTION:**

The world is facing many challenges with no solution in sight.

The main cause of all these ills is the POVERTY. Float bonds which can be used by everybody rich or poor and are not debt to the state so there is no question of interest.

*How*: Take the example of INDIA which is going through a great recession.

INDIA borrows money by selling treasury bills and the interest based bonds. The suggestion is to sell these bonds on non interest basis.

1. Buy all goods and services under Government control with these bonds and these bonds will replace Rupees with bonds.
2. At least 200 billion euro remitted in less than 30 days when duty free option on 10 million Rs. is waved of if 1000 Euro is remitted (non refundable) within the first 30 days of implementing the system.
3. RS.100 billion prize draw from the bonds bought by the public every day.

EXAMPLE: ONE Rupee will buy 6 bonds on the condition that the amount should be RS.100000 or multiple of it paid to the government and the government will issue 600000 bonds. Fewer amounts will get the rate of five, four and three. This MASSIVE discount period is only for first month at the start of the implementation of this system. In the second month the rate will be 5 and in the third month the rate will be 4 but the rate of 3 will apply to subsequent months for the same amount.

*WHERE THESE BONDS WILL BE USED?*

1. All state controlled services and commodities.

*EXAMPLE*: A bill of (any service or Commodity) RS.100 can be paid with 200 bonds and there will be no exception to this rule. A NET DISCOUNT OF 66%.

A simple formula will apply: Total bill in Rupees x2 is the number of bonds surrendered. Price in bonds will not be less than the cost price but without the direct indirect taxes and the duties which are added to the present cost to make it very expensive.

It will attract at least 240 million people to take this opportunity as early as possible. And if one is sure of making 100% profit within 30 days there will be many more that will help themselves.

**RESULT: Government gets at least Rs. 50 trillion within a very short period of time of few days and much more in the rest of the year. THIS IS NOT A DEBT AS STATE HAS SOLD BONDS (Commodity) WHICH IS AN ALTERNATE CURRENCY AND DO NOT CARRY ANY INTEREST**. One immediately thinks who will bear the loss and this loss to the state will not be more than total year budget which it collects in one year with all the taxes and the duties but the bond price is simply a cost price without any kind of tax or duty. So there is a net gain of approximately 50 trillion Rupees within a short period of time. First floodgate of money has been opened.

*WHO WILL SELL THESE BONDS?*

State will float tenders to select a private agency (INMF) INDIA MONITORY FUND JUST A NAME GIVEN TO THIS ORGANIZATION with the lowest bid WHERE AS second, third and fourth bidders will be auditors of INMF. This agency will employ at least 50 million unemployed on 10% commission basis and without any salary. These agents will have to pay Rs. 5000 as an annual fee to INMF in order to build the infrastructure for the sale of bonds. Agents' quota will be Rs. 300,000 per month or they will be allowed to sell their whole year quota in one day or in a month. This will only materialize if the agent shares his commission with the buyer. Greater the share of commission quicker the sale. The investor or a buyer will sell these bonds at the same rate of 6 per Rupees and his bonds will sell like hot cakes every day as there is no condition of the amount of money to purchase the bonds. In this way even the poorest person will get the same or near the same rate as the investor earns a profit from the commission which he takes from the agent and makes almost 100% profit by only investing Rs. 100,000. He will sell these bonds repeatedly and will keep almost 6% profit every day till the demand lasts. ***NOW THINK HOW MUCH FUNDS***

***STATE HAS ACCUMULATED Much more than few years budget in matter of only one month.***

**FLOOD GATES OF MONEY AND TURNING POINT**

This is the second flood gate of money and there are still four more floodgates of money yet to open. So at the end of 30 days or even much earlier the government declares tax free country forever.

With the removal of all kinds of direct and indirect taxes and duties the price of oil electricity telephone and of all other services under government control is now almost 66% less than before as these are being purchased by bonds (which is the cost price) and not with Rupees. The production cost of everything has come down tremendously.

**SECOND OPTION**

***STATE ALSO OFFERS 10 MILLION DUTY FREE IF ONE DEPOSITS 1000 EURO NON REFUNDABLE. THIS BRINGS OUT ALL THE BLACK AND SPARE MONEY WHICH STATE WAS NOT ABLE TO GET BEFORE AND AS THERE IS NO TAX AND HENCE NO TAX EVASION SO ALL THE MONEY IS WHITE AS IT IS BEING GIVEN TO GOVERNMENT. This is the third flood gate of money and the amount will much bigger than the first two flood gates***

This was the third floodgate of money which is even bigger than the first one and the exact amount is impossible to asses unless the system is implemented.

**In order to provide cheap bonds throughout the year government offers three types of registration fees.**

1. Pay Rs. 10,000 in the start of the year and get the rate of 6 for the rest of the year and this will suit the professional's and salaried person'

2. Pay RS.10,000 yearly and get 20,000 new bonds at the rate 6 every month but one has to collect 10,000 bonds (equal to fee) to get this cheap rate throughout the year. Higher the registration fee more the entitlement of cheap bonds. This registration will suit any small time business who will sell his product cheaper provided 15% bonds are also paid with rest of cash money by the customer SEE THE NEXT REGISTRATION FOR FURTHER EXPLANATION OF 15%BONDS. This will apply to all goods in private sector and does not apply to the government sector. This is a big incentive to accept bonds in the private sector as the business accepting more bonds will have more business than the trader not accepting the bonds so the bonds market will multiply and there will be a constant need for bonds in the open market.

3. Third type of registration will be of Rs. 100,000 which will entitle the business to sell its products through INMF. The value of merchandise sold through this source will help the business to get the 6 bond per Rupees rate or opt for the duty free option equal the amount sold. But with one condition of surrendering 15% bonds at each transaction

EXAMPLE:

MERCHANDISED SOLD THROUGH INMF RS.1000. BONDS SURRENDERED 150 (15 %) ARE DEPOSITED IN STATE ACCOUNT TO BE SOLD AGAIN SO THE CYCLE OF BONDS IS ESTABLISHED. A receipt of bonds surrendered is obtained from INMF for evidence of sale of merchandise and this receipt will entitle the traders to get cheap bonds or the duty free option throughout the year BUT THE SAME RECEIPT CAN BE USED ONCE ONLY.

## WHAT IS THE BENEFIT TO BUSINESS?

1. CHEAP BONDS THROUGH OUT THE YEAR
2. DUTY FREE OPTION WILL HELP INDUSTRY.

3. The quota which can be sold is ten times the amount of Registration but not more unless the registration fee is increased. Now all the business will opt for this registration in order to reduce the cost of production. These 15% bonds the business will get back through a chain of dealers sub dealers and ultimately the customer will pay this bond portion as he will get the end product very cheap because of tremendous cut in the cost of production by the factors already mentioned. This will replace the GST or the VAT or the two price system seen all over INDIA. Almost everybody will sell their product through this channel as it will be much costlier to sell the product outside this system as cheap bonds are not available otherwise.

According to rough estimate at least RS.100 trillion transactions are carried out every day in India and at each transaction 15% bonds are being surrendered, the price of 15 bonds is Rs. 2.5. So 2.5% of 100 trillion will be Rs. 2.5 trillion which goes into government account without any compulsion every day (UNBELIEVABLE). ***This is the Fourth floodgate of money AND IS CALLED THE GOLD MINE.*** Now the state is sitting in the driving seat and all the money in banks of private sector has been transferred into government account and banks are no more the lenders but are borrower from the state which is the only source left and will invest in business with sound feasibility study checked by the state bank. The state will offer to invest 80% and the bank will bring investor who is willing to pool rest 20%. This 20% will be deposited in the bank and the bank will oversee the running the business, running expenses will be given to the investor from its share of 20%. There will be no collateral and share of the profit and loss will be shared in the ratio of 60 and 40. The bank will share the 60% with the investor and 40% will go to state funds and the state will provide everything under its control below cost which will farther reduce the cost of production and at the same time will MARKEDLY improve the profit margins OF ALL THE BUSINESSES. No major business can refuse this offer. Any bank showing repeated loss will go out of business as there will be no more funds available from the government source and all other interest based sources are not available any more. Interest based banking is gone forever or it may be at a very small scale and the state will not offer loans on interest as these are not any more profitable and risk free as there is no collateral. ***The amount of profit government will share will be unimaginable and this is the 5th flood gate opened.***

## THEN WHY NOT INVEST ON PROFIT AND LOSS SHARING BASIS

Last but not the least government will acquire all the land on lease without any force and will provide all the needs to the formers ***THROUGH CORPORATE FARMING SECTOR HIRED BY THE STATE below cost and will become the shareholder according to the mutual contract with the land owner this is the 6th flood gate of*** money opened.

**DRUG ABUSE ELIMINATED**

When all the possible land is being cultivated by best agriculture engineers there will be much better yield and much more profit to land owner then who will not join hands with the government.

THE OBVIOUS BENEFIT WILL BE NO MORE POPPY CULTIVATION IN COUNTRIES WHICH ARE POOR AND LARGELY DEPEND ON THE POPPY CROP. NOW THERE IS NO MORE POPPY AND NO MORE DRUGS.

| MY ANALYSIS AND PREDICTION ABOUT US ECONOMY |
|---|
| The U.S economy is like a giant oak tree that has rotten roots, hollow stems, and dying leaves, and it is quite possible that this mighty tree will fall and bury every nation relaxing under its shade. MBCS is the fertilizer that can bring the U.S. economic tree back to life. |
| This prediction is available on internet and written in a book titled ISLAMIC ECONOMIC REVOLUTION OF THE CENTURY published in USA and UK in 2006 |

# CHAPTER 1

## INTRODUCTION

There is nothing certain but death and taxes. Since the earliest days of human history, governments have collected taxes. Ancient, Chinese, Egyptian, and Indian farmers and European feudal serfs paid tithes on their lands. With the rise of the middle classes, accountable governments have levied taxes on incomes, goods, capital and wealth, inheritance, and even windows. Although taxes are an inevitable part of life, societies have had to solve several problems associated with obtaining the money needed to run their governments and maintain their infrastructures: how much money to collect, how to collect it, where to collect it, who will collect it, and how to spend it. Some societies have used religion to guide their tax collection and laws, and other societies have used pragmatism and common sense to create the procedures for collecting taxes and establish laws.

While everyone pays taxes, ordinary, often poorer citizens who cannot pay for good tax advice carry the largest tax burden. From their ranks come the teachers, engineers, doctors, nurses, lawyers, scientists, and other high-value citizens without whom most societies would be so much poorer. It seems unfair that the people who contribute the most to a society's well-being are forced to carry the largest tax load. Modern-day people would be much better off if they lived in a tax-free society.

A world without taxes would be a paradise to many people, but it seems unimaginable, a pipe dream, an illusion. It seems an impossible dream to find a system that eliminates taxes; however, using the mutual benefit Bond system (MBCS), it is possible to create a tax-free world. Although people may laugh at the idea of a tax-free world, many people also laughed at the idea of landing astronauts on the moon, splitting the atom, or curing diseases. Using MBCS, it is possible to

1. abolish all taxes,
2. fund governments in new and productive ways,
3. create incentives for rich and poor citizens,
4. promote sensible public and private investment,
5. make governments more accountable for spending,
6. improve the quality of life for all people, and
7. Eliminate poverty and illiteracy and the social ills caused by them.

Although MBCS seems like another fad, another 5-minute wonder, it is a system that can achieve this utopian ideal.

**MBCS is based on incentive based principles, and it is designed to:**

1. eliminate unfair financial burdens from all sectors of society;
2. remove taxes, duties, and levies;
3. revolutionize government revenue collection and liquidity;
4. eliminate poverty;
5. rebuild national infrastructures;
6. restore law and order; and
7. Provide all citizens with equal opportunities.

This book describes MBCS and how it works. It discusses the weaknesses of the present taxation system and its adverse effect on the lives of billions of people. The World Bank and International Monetary Fund (IMF) and their effect on the economies of developing countries are examined. This book compares MBCS applied on Indian economy and present financial instruments.

**There is a discussion about the role of the interest free banking system when MBCS is instituted, and a description**

of how different countries collect taxes. In addition, this book explains how MBCS can help eliminate the drug trade, terrorism, poverty, taxes and reverse recession in matter of days with a massive jump start in the economy of every country implementing this system.

## CHAPTER 2

# MBCS (MUTUAL BENEFIT BOND SYSTEM) HOW MBCS WORKS: A CASE STUDY OF INDIA

MBCS is a simple system. In this system, all goods and services under government control are offered to end users and consumers at two prices. The first price is the current or prevailing market price and includes all types of taxes and duties a government collect to meet its budget requirements. This price is much higher than the price offered through MBCS, and it includes most of the taxes and duties. The second price is much lower than current market price because it is offered at almost cost price by the government if purchased by Bonds and not Rupee at the cheapest price (i.e., six Bonds per Rupee) So it all depends on the price of MBCS Bond at the time of purchase. This lower price is the incentive for consumers and end users to participate in MBCS.

In order to obtain this lower price, the buyer has to pay for a commodity or service under government control with a certain number of MBCS Bonds. The number of Bonds will be shown on the bill provided by the government authority. In addition, the bill will also show the current prevailing price. The reduced price can be easily calculated by the purchaser because it will always be double the amount of Bonds of the current price in Rupees: For example, 10 Rupees is the present price, which can be paid by 20 Bonds. The number of Bonds will be two times the amount of Rupees. Two prices are used in MBCS in order to calculate the bond price of a commodity or service. In addition, the current price is kept because it shows how expensive a good or service would cost if a consumer decides not to use MBCS Bonds. The savings to the buyer can range from 20% to 60% or more, depending on the rate of Bond. As a result, the consumer gets more for less.

In addition to lower prices, MBCS encourages buyers to participate in the scheme by offering discounts on bulk buys of Bonds. As a result, a buyer can establish a price for a commodity or service by timing the purchase of Bonds to take advantage of discounts. These discounts also include allowances for duty-free imports instead of cheap Bonds or both, and they are offered in the first, second, and third months of a financial year. After the discount period expires, the rate will be fixed (3 Bond per Rupee) for the rest of the year.

MBCS Bonds would be available from a non government organization (NGO) and its agents, and the name of this agency will depend on the government. For example, in India, this agency could be called the India Monetary Fund (INMF). Organizations would bid for the right to sell Bonds, and the agency selected to operate the monetary fund would employ agents about 50 to 100 million unemployed and on social security at present. They would receive a 10% commission on all Bond sales and there will be a fixed quota for a year for each agent. The organization with the lowest bid and the ability to put the scheme into operation in the shortest time would receive the contract. The second-, third-, or fourth-lowest bidders as well as the government would audit the monetary fund. These auditors would work independently on a fixed fee paid by the monetary fund plus a 50% penalty imposed on INMF, which would be 10 times the amount of any discrepancy or fraud. The government would receive the remaining 50% of the penalty.

**No rational business, organization, or individual can afford to ignore this scheme if it is offered; therefore, it is reasonable to assume the following:**

1. People, businesses, and organizations will purchase large quantities of Bonds.
2. They will purchase them in the early part of the year in order to take advantage of discounts.
3. Bonds will be purchased for a number of reasons other than simply paying bills: for example, saving Bonds, speculating

in sales later in the year, and holding Bonds as a hedge against unexpected expenses.
4. Bonds will be used at every opportunity to reduce the cost of producing goods and services, from government imports to the point of sale to the end user.

In addition to lower costs, MBCS would include lucky draws (Rs. 100 billion) everyday, which are like a lottery but without any cost to a person. These draws would encourage people to hold their Bonds in the hopes of winning the draw. As a result, the government would have more money than expected because Bonds are not being used, the government is not paying interest on the money collected as it is not a loan, and they would not be recalled unless the value drops below a certain level. If the value drops below (6 per Rupee) a certain level, the government would buy back the Bonds at a low rate in order to increase the value of the Bonds.

**MBCS has a number of benefits for a government that is having problems collecting enough revenue to meet its needs:**

1. At the beginning of each year, the monetary fund would offer MBCS Bonds for sale without restriction. MBCS Bonds would cover all government-controlled goods and services throughout the entire economic chain; therefore, there should be a large demand for these Bonds. The cash raised by the sale of these Bonds would go straight to the government through the monetary fund. In many developing countries, the initial sale of Bonds will produce enough funds to cover the financial needs of a government for several years because the underground economy will merge with the mainstream economy.

2. In this scheme, a government takes the lead in price reductions by discounting fuel, electricity, telephones, and so forth, which would reduce household, agricultural, and industrial costs. This would have a significant, positive impact on economic activity because a reduction in the prices of all essential goods and services with free imports

would bring down factory prices and, at the same time, increase profitability, which will be an attractive incentive for new investment.
3. A government would benefit from increased liquidity, investment, and economic activity. In addition, as the economy grows, the government would sell more Bonds.
4. This new economy is attractive to all parties, and people engaged in the black economy found in many developing countries will migrate to MBCS. It will no longer be attractive to work outside the system because it will be impossible to compete with it on price.

MBCS is a unique, risk-free approach to raising revenue for governments. It does not require a government to give up its current system of revenue generation until MBCS proves that it is capable of raising enough money to meet a government's needs. Once the system is in place, it will transform dysfunctional economies often found in the developing world into open, transparent, free markets in which the government and citizens co-operate to drive prices down, create surplus budgets, and increase investment. Once a government has accumulated more than enough money to run the country for a year, it would announce a complete tax holiday in which no further income tax would be imposed on any person or businesses. This is the starting point for an industrial revolution.

## MBCS IN INDIA: A CASE STUDY

India is currently facing many challenges, but its most important challenge is improving the financial credibility of its government. According to the **2014** *CIA World Fact book*. India is developing into an open-market economy, yet traces of its past autarkic policies remain. Economic liberalization measures, including industrial deregulation, privatization of state-owned enterprises, and reduced controls on foreign trade and investment, began in the early 1990s and have served to accelerate the country's growth, which averaged under 7% per year since 1997. India's diverse economy encompasses traditional village farming, modern agriculture, handicrafts, a wide range of modern industries, and a multitude of services. Slightly more than half of the work force is in agriculture, but services are the major source of economic growth, accounting for nearly two-thirds of India's output, with less than one-third of its labor force. India has capitalized on its large educated English-speaking population to become a major exporter of information technology services, business outsourcing services, and software workers. In 2010, the Indian economy rebounded robustly from the global financial crisis - in large part because of strong domestic demand - and growth exceeded 8% year-on-year in real terms. However, India's economic growth began slowing in 2011 because of a slowdown in government spending and a decline in investment, caused by investor pessimism about the government's commitment to further economic reforms and about the global situation. High international crude prices have exacerbated the government's fuel subsidy expenditures, contributing to a higher fiscal deficit and a worsening current account deficit. In late 2012, the Indian Government announced additional reforms and deficit reduction measures to reverse India's slowdown, including allowing higher levels of foreign participation in direct investment in the economy. The outlook for India's medium-term growth is positive due to a young population and corresponding low dependency ratio, healthy savings and investment rates, and increasing integration into the global economy. India has many long-term challenges that it has yet to fully address, including poverty, corruption, violence and discrimination against women and girls, an inefficient power generation and distribution system, ineffective enforcement of intellectual property rights, decades-long civil litigation dockets, inadequate transport and agricultural infrastructure, limited non-agricultural employment opportunities, inadequate availability of quality basic and higher education, and accommodating rural-to-urban migration.

Increasingly, the ability of Indian government (GOI) to carry out a program of reform and embark on a program of targeted expenditure on the infrastructure has been limited by the parlous state of the economy. The root cause of many of these problems is India's taxation system. The government cannot collect enough money from taxation to fulfill its promises and obligations. As a result, the taxation system in India has fallen into disrepute, and its inability to raise enough money to meet the government's needs threatens India's future. Table 1 shows the extent to which the system has failed and how massive debt has eroded the solvency of India's government.

| Revenue | 2010 | 2011 | 2012 | 2013 | 2014 | % change |
|---|---|---|---|---|---|---|
| Total revenue | $170 b | $ 181. b | $ 176.2b | $181.3 b | $198 b | More than 15% |
| Total Expenditures | $257.4b | $205.7b | $244b | $281.6 b | $ 292 b | More than 15% |

b = billion dollars

### India's Current Economic System

The following definitions describe India's current economic system:

**Cost:** Cost is the actual expenses incurred manufacturing goods or producing services. It includes:

1. Manufacturing/production expenses,
2. Raw material costs,
3. Custom duties and other levies paid on imports, and
4. Conversion costs (i.e., price of electricity, telephone service, gas, and all types of taxes and levies charged during the production process)

**Price:** Price is the selling price of any commodity or service that includes the cost of a good or service plus profit (i.e., Cost + Profit = Price).

The Indian tax system is complicated. Most people find it difficult to understand, and the Indian government spends millions of Rupees every year collecting taxes. MBCS would eliminate this complicated system and enable the United States to spend the money used to collect taxes on more useful projects. Although tax consultants would not be necessary in MBCS, they would be able to find employment in this system.

**The following list of taxes shows that the India tax system is quite complex:**

1. <u>Corporate Taxation:</u> Corporate profits are taxed at a corporate tax rate, and dividends paid to shareholders are taxed at a separate rate. This system is called double taxation because corporate profits paid to shareholders are taxed twice.

2. <u>Individual Taxation:</u> Wages and salaries, pensions, bonuses, commissions, business income, dividends, interest, capital gains, rent, and royalties are taxed in India. Taxes are also collected for any overseas investments of an Indian citizen. In addition, Indian citizens and residents must pay an estate tax on inheritances.

3. <u>International Company Taxation:</u> Indian companies that operate overseas must pay taxes on their profits. The laws concerning these taxes are very complex and require professional help to avoid penalties.

As described in chapter 2, MBCS is an incentive-based system that will greatly reduce the cost of living for average people and reduce production costs for businesses. It will also produce more than enough money for the Indian government to balance its budgets and eliminate its debts. Table 18 shows the effects MBCS will have on the India's financial situation.

**Table 18. The Effects of MBCS on the India's Financial Situation**

| Current System (amount in billions) | MBCS (amount in billions) |
|---|---|
| total budget = $ 292 billion | projected budget = up to $ 1 trillion |
| unemployment = 8.5 % | unemployment = 0% |
| current debt (approx) = $ 440 billion | total debt = INR0.00 |
| current VAT on retail sales = 15% | government-controlled aid = 3% (gives incentive) |
| inflation @ 6.46 % per annum (approx) | total deflation |
| industrial production growth rate = 1.2% | industrial production growth rate above 100% |
| black money runs into trillions of Rupees | no black money |

**India's Economic System under MBCS**

The following definitions describe India's economic system under MBCS:

**Rupee Value:** Rupee value is a current prevailing market price. This price is not applicable to consumers and is only used to calculate the numbers of Bonds needed to purchase a good or service. According to the most conservative estimates, if all the indirect taxes were abolished, production cost would be reduced by 50%. This reduced cost, which includes actual cost and profit, is the Rupee value in MBCS.

**Bond Value:** The MBCS Bond value is the price of goods and services, which is twice the value of a current Rupee value.

**Bond:** A MBCS Bond replaces all indirect taxes, custom duties, excise taxes, surcharges, and all other levies. The cheaper the Bond, the less tax paid by a consumer or business.

**Actual Price:** In MBCS, the actual selling price is the price a subscriber or consumer has to pay, and this price depends on the cost of Bonds. The cheaper the Bond, the cheaper the price of the commodity or service provided by the government.

**Production Cost:** In MBCS, production costs will be reduced by 50% because all direct and indirect taxes, duties, surcharges, and other levies are abolished and replaced by Bonds. These taxes are eliminated because the government is able to collect enough money within a few days of implementing MBCS to meets it annual budget.

In India (Total population 1200 million) 20% of the population (i.e., 240 million people) can easily spend 100,000 Rupees in the first few days to reduce their daily bills by two thirds of the previous cost. This will raise INR 24 trillion for the government, which is more than enough money to meet the government's budgetary needs. (Budget 2014-15 is Rs17.95 trillion= $ 292 billion) Once this money is raised, India would be declared a tax-free heaven, even for the foreign investor. This is one of the doors through which money will flood into Govt.'s treasury. There are five more doors through which money will flow to the government, and these will be described later in this chapter.

**Philosophy of MBCS**

In MBCS, a current prevailing market price is the India Rupee value, and the other price is the Bond value. The Bond value is a subsidized price, with an average discount of 40% to 66% compared to the prevailing market price. The price of a Bond will vary between two and six Bonds per Rupees, depending on the amount purchased, time of purchase, or whether they are purchased under special registration rules (up to six Bonds per Rupee during the whole year, depending on the type of registration).

These Bonds will reduce the cost of production by at least 50%, which will reduce the cost of living. This reduced price will not be below the actual cost of a good or service and will carry at least a 10% mark-up on the cost price provided by the government.

In MBCS, it is possible for businesses to use a duty-free option. It would increase the import of technically and extremely useful high-tech industry products more than 10 times the present rate. MBCS would also increase all other types of imports because of the demand and supply factor. This duty-free environment would not hurt the government because all these imports would be carried out by the private sector, and the only role played by the government would be the removal of these unnecessary duties. As a result of the duties, the private sector imports goods from neighboring countries where these products are cheaper than they would be if Indian businesses tried to produce them. In MBCS, the duty on fuel would be almost nonexistent.

**Tax as a Burden**

In 2014, the Government of India collected INR 11.9 trillion ($192 billion) in direct and indirect taxes. This is equal to INR1491.66 for every man, woman, and child in India (*CIA Country Yearbook*, 2014).

1. These people are gainfully employed, and many of them are owner/managers or professionals. (Private Sector)
2. Income tax is paid by at least 15 to 20 % of population but everybody pays indirect taxes.

Given that the per capita Gross Domestic Product (GDP) of India is $3,800 the tax burden being carried by this small group of taxpayers is absurd.

**Why MBCS Can Work for India**

India's current revenue system requires indirect taxes, import duties, government duties, and price controls. In addition, higher prices for controlled goods and services, as a means of collecting revenue in an economy that is under performing even with the help of very high taxes is unpopular.

In order to create a successful revenue collection system in India, it is necessary to ensure that the revenue net is spread as far as possible, and there must be a general consensus among those within the net that co-operation is worthwhile.

**The Tax Position in India**

Several features of the India tax environment are pertinent to MBCS:

1. A previous attempt to institute a broad-based sales tax on consumption failed because it was unpopular. In India, 29 % of the population lives below the poverty line (World Bank, 2014), and taxing the poor, albeit indirectly, is deeply resented and politically dangerous.

2. India has, as conceded by the World Bank and the U.S. government (*CIA World Fact book*, 2014), one of the most promising economies in South Asia. In the mid-to-late 1990s, it was capable of significant GDP growth (i.e., 7%–7.6% per annum) under the right circumstances.

The existing tax system has failed to retire India's debt and provide the funds needed to improve the country's infrastructure. MBCS would generate enough money to retire the debt and improve the standard of living for everyone living in India.

**Changing the Indian Mindset**

MBCS provides a revenue collection system for the Government of India, and it is based on a nationwide, dual pricing system for all goods and services and associated profits. This applies not only to Govt.-controlled goods and services, but also to goods and services provided by the private sector.

In order to enjoy lower prices, citizens prepay for a MBCS Bond that is used for buying goods and services that have two prices. The revenue from the sale of these Bonds goes to the government through a national monetary fund that sells Bonds and collects money. In India, this national organization would be called the India Monetary Fund (a private contractor) (INMF), and it would pay revenue collected from the sale of Bonds directly to Govt. accounts.

MBCS is a revenue system, not a tax system. In effect, the scheme asks businesses and consumers to help the government, and it encourages people to use this system by offering lower prices for goods and services. MBCS is attractive to consumers because it appeals to people's desire to find the best deal for a good or service.

**MBCS' Economic Appeal**

In MBCS, there is no statutory obligation to buy Bonds. The scheme relies entirely on the basic human instinct of getting the best deal for the money. Unlike India's current indirect tax system, MBCS will attract people because it offers guaranteed discounts on goods and services.

The lower prices available with MBCS Bonds will attract at least 20% of the population. In addition, it will attract consumers because they will pay a higher price (present price) without Bonds. MBCS will eventually attract enough participants to enable India to eliminate its current indirect tax system. In addition, because Bonds will be bought at the start of a financial year, the government will know exactly how much money it will have to fulfill its obligations during the year.

**A MICROECONOMIC CASE FOR MBCS**

MBCS will affect the micro economy of India in the following ways:

1. All transactions involving the use of money or credit for goods and services can operate under the scheme. (Govt. Sector)
2. MBCS applies to the entire economy, including non profit organisations.
3. MBCS will reduce household and business costs, which will increase consumer net disposable income (NDI) and business profitability.
4. MBCS will have an immediate, favorable impact on economic activity, employment, and government revenues.
5. MBCS will affect the supply (e.g., imports, manufacturing, agriculture, and services) and demand (e.g., individuals, households, and business) sides of India's economy and eliminate supply/demand curve imbalances.
6. MBCS revenues will reflect the level of economic activity in the macro economy, and the system will grow proportionately with the growth of GDP.
7. MBCS incentives will reduce the need for a large bank balance and encourage more people to participate in the open economy as Bond accounts will be much more profitable than interest based accounts.

**MBCS in Outline**

In MBCS, an Indian consumer would use a prepaid Bond (i.e., in the form of a plastic card/voucher) when purchasing any goods or service (under Govt. Control). The consumer who uses a Bond would be entitled to significant discounts on the listed sales price/cost of utility bills and other purchases.

While the scheme requires the government to discount, in some cases, its indirect tax rate/fixed pricing to people using Bonds, it will increase upfront cash flows to the government. The short-, medium-, and long-term benefits of increased and timely revenue collection will far outweigh a theoretical reduction in indirect tax rates/price controls.

MBSC will work in the favor of consumers, and businesses will gain significant, preferential advantages by using Bonds. Businesses will be drawn into the scheme by the simple pressure of lower prices offered by businesses that participate in MBCS.

MBCS will increase India's GDP, and this will substantially outweigh the discount aspect of the system. In addition, MBCS will cause massive foreign currency outside India to migrate into MBCS-based transactions and increase Govt.'s revenue .Net (see Figure 1).

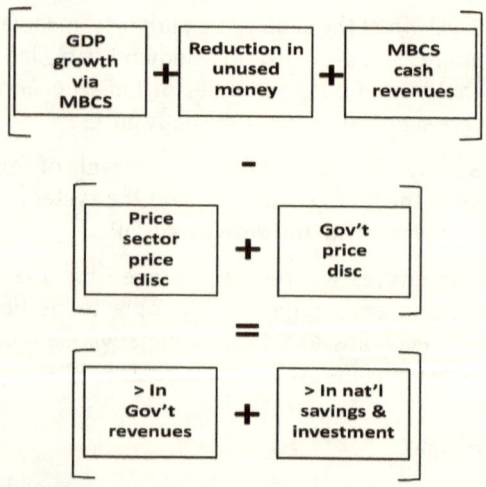

**Figure 1. Economic Impact of MBCS**

**Why Price Controls?**

India controls the prices of a large number of critical items:

1. Electricity;
2. Petrol, diesel, and aviation fuel;
3. Telecommunication services;
4. Road taxes;

5. A large range of consumer items;
6. Registration fees, stamp duties, and other government fees & license fees;
7. Court fees;
8. Fixed duties on air travel;
9. Surcharges on airline tickets;
10. Road taxes;
11. Import duties;
12. Property taxes;
13. Post office fees;
14. Fees for passports and identity cards.
15. Marriage duties;
16. Fees for private educational institutes and private and government hospitals; and
17. Fees on all applications to government offices and agencies.

Govt. controls prices for a number of reasons, but it primarily controls prices in order to supplement its indirect tax revenues with profits from the sale of price-controlled goods and services. In fact, it is the only way it can guarantee it will collect revenue on certain items because a general sales tax is neither practical nor politically acceptable. MBCS would enable the Government of India to continue the practice of making money directly from sales, and it would model the two-tiered price scheme for the private sector by offering a discount price to consumers who use MBCS Bonds. Figure 2 compares current costs for Govt.-controlled goods and services and savings under MBCS.

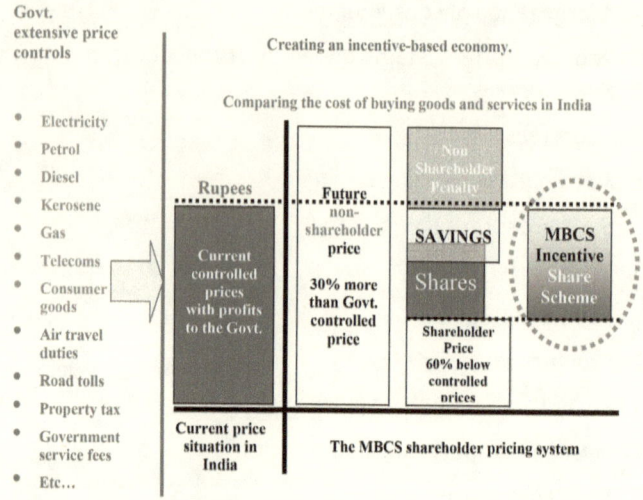

Figure 2. Comparing Costs in India's Current System and MBCS

## MBCS and Incentives

In the beginning, the government would offer its priced-controlled items at two prices: India Rupee value and Bond value. The Bond price is lower than the Rupee price, which will become artificial price, and it offers a considerable advantage over the artificial price in real cash terms. In order to enjoy the lower price, consumers would pay twice as many Bonds as Rupees for the same good or service. This appears to be a win-win situation for consumers if Bonds are bought at a rate below face value (e.g., six Bonds per Rupee or even three or four Bonds per Rupee), consumers would save at least 20%, even if the rate was three Bonds per Indian Rupee. However, in the open market, the rate of Bonds per Rupee would always be above three Bonds per Rupee. (See Figure 3).

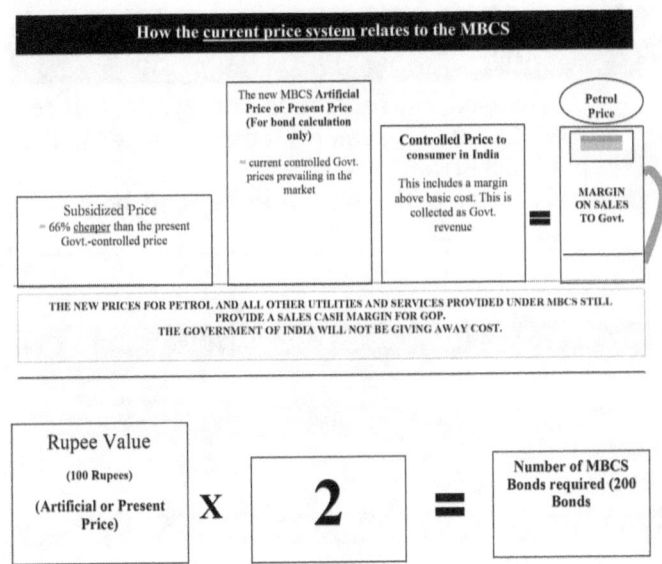

Figure 3. Current Price System's Relationship to MBCS

## MBCS Prices

In MBCS, there are two stated prices and one final price (see Figure 4):

1. The first stated price is the artificial price, called Rupee value (stated on label/list). This price is used only to calculate the number of MBCS Bonds required and will be the prevailing market price.

2. The second price is the with-Bond price, called Bond value (stated on label/list). This price is 40% to 60% lower than current prices and will (depending on the Bond rate per Rupee at the time) show how many **Bonds are needed for the purchase.**

3. The third and final price is the actual price in INR. This is the price in Rupees actually paid by the consumer once the number of Bonds is calculated.

### WHY DOES THE ACTUAL PRICE VARY SO MUCH? HOW DO I KNOW WHAT I'M PAYING?

- When paying for goods and services under MBCS, the consumer is most interested in **the Actual Price**
- **So what is the Actual Price, and how is it calculated?**

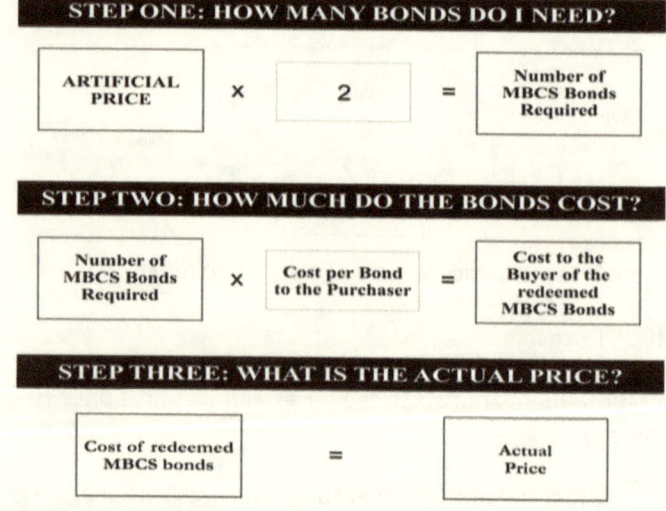

**Figure 4. Calculating Actual Price**

**Calculating the Cost of Bonds**

It is quite easy to calculate the cost of MBCS Bonds: More Bonds equal lower costs, and earlier Bond purchases in a financial year equals more benefits. The incentive to participate in MBCS is lower prices for goods and services. In addition, consumers are rewarded for buying more Bonds early in a financial year. Table 2 shows the benefits of buying Bonds in bulk: For example, a consumer could spend from 0.05 Rupee to 0.167 Rupee per Bond, depending on the time of year the Bonds are purchased.

## Table 2. Benefits of Buying Bonds in Bulk

| Month | | Official Bond Cost | Open Market Rate |
|---|---|---|---|
| 1 | January | 100% of special concession* | 3 to 6 per Rupee depending upon the availability of number of Bonds |
| 2 | February | 70% of special concession* | |
| 3 | March | 50% of special concession* | |
| 4 | April | | |
| 5 | May | | |
| 6 | June | Bonds available on the market at the rates set out in Official tables | |
| 7 | July | | |
| 8 | August | | |
| 9 | September | | |
| 10 | October | (Lowest exchange rate) | |
| 11 | November | | |
| 12 | December | | |

*During the first financial quarter of each year, MBCS would operate under a special concession arrangement to encourage the maximum upfront purchase of Bonds. The concession enables any person, household, or business to buy at a rate of six Bonds per Indian Rupee in the first month, which is the maximum amount, and will keep on decreasing over time.

## The Rationale for a Sliding Scale for Bond Costs

The financial objective of MBCS is to deliver substantial upfront revenues (i.e., liquidity) to Govt. and improve its solvency (e.g., balanced budgets). MBCS uses a sliding scale to encourage people to buy large quantities of Bonds early in a financial year. There are four reasons to use a sliding scale for Bond costs:

1. A sliding scale encourages people to buy large quantities of Bonds in the first month of a financial year;
2. It encourages the largest possible sales in single transactions.
3. It encourages non-bank deposits to buy Bonds.
4. It rewards the good customer.

The sliding scale has several implications for consumers:

1. Consumers with large cash deposits, whether in or out of the official economy, will be encouraged to buy large quantities of Bonds. The Bonds will have significant value to high-, middle-, and low-income households because MBCS Bonds will be used to purchase all goods and services, from luxuries to necessities.

2. Bonds are bearer entitled, and the holder of a Bond will enjoy its benefits. Therefore, Bonds can be traded on the open market and sold at a profit.

3. Buyers of Bonds can trade in futures by taking options from traders on their future requirements at mutually agreed rates. This is particularly important because Bonds will be available through official channels at their best rates only during the early part of a financial year; however, consumers who can buy more than INR 800,000 worth of Bonds would be able to obtain a rate of 5 Bonds per Rupee throughout the year.

4. The costs of living and production will be reduced and create consumer demand, savings, and increased profit.

**Figure 5. Sliding Scale for Bond Costs**

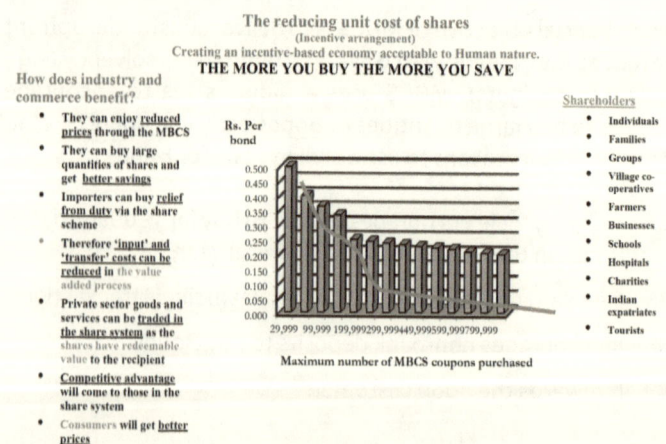

**Reasons for Purchasing MBCS Bonds**

There are three reasons why a consumer would want to purchase MBCS Bonds:

1. Bond-based transactions are less expensive than Rupee-based transactions.
2. Bonds purchased at the beginning of a financial year are less expensive than Bonds purchased later in the year.
3. The cheaper the Bonds, the cheaper the price of the goods and services bought using Bonds.
4. Daily 100 billion Rupees prize draw will be a huge attraction.
5. At least 100 % return within 30 days and more in later months.

The best deals (i.e., rates for Bonds) will come through official channels during the first financial quarter. This will attract substantial revenues ahead of purchasing requirements, and it will be a win-win situation for the Government of India and consumers.

The more expensive official Bond market in the remainder of a financial year will encourage open market trading among businesses and individuals who trade Bond surpluses for shortfalls at negotiated prices. This market is important because it creates a broad-based value for an exchange market that is independent of Govt. price controls. This will further support the growth of the Bond system in the open market.

Banks and financial institutions will be able to trade through their normal distribution channels and provide MBCS Bond accounts as well as normal Indian Rupee cash and deposit accounts. Banks will also be able to purchase larger quantities of Bonds in the early part of a financial year on a speculative basis and offer these Bonds to their customers during the year. Banks can top up customer Bond accounts at agreed rates and times. This trade in Bonds will be a very lucrative business for banks and a valuable customer service.

Approximately at-least 80% of India's population pays for the basics of modern living, such as telephones, gas, water, electricity, and so forth. MBCS will offer cheaper actual prices on the consumption of these important everyday basics. The following steps show how the price for a basic commodity is calculated using MBCS:

1. When calculating the bill for a commodity, the vendor uses present prevailing tariff charges.
2. When the bill is paid, Bonds will replace Rupees and the savings will depend on the rate of Bonds when they were purchased. Utility bills will calculate/show the number of Bonds required by the user, so there will be no confusion or need for the consumer to do the calculating.
3. The Bond value price of the utility will be much lower than the Rupee value price.

Figures 6, 7, and 8 show how MBCS affects the price of electricity for large, medium, and small consumers. Table 3 shows the cost of petrol under MBCS.

(These are MBCS Prices of 2014; the prices are different for the Residential, Commercial and Industrial sectors. The average cost is Rs. 5/KWH in India)

| India Electricity Billing Authority (Reg. Under MBCS) ||||
|---|---|---|---|
| | Calculations | | Costs in INR | Bonds |
| 1 | Units last reading | 12500 | | |
| 2 | Units this reading | 13500 | | |
| 3 | Units consumed* | 1000 | | |
| 4 | **INR** Value Price | suppose | 1000 | |
| 5 | Bond Value Price | | | 10,000 |
| 6 | Bonds required | | | 10,000 |

| | | | Bonds |
|---|---|---|---|
| Total MBCS Bonds to pay bill | | | **10,000** |
| *Existing electricity tariff cost to consumer (2014) | INR. 5000 | | Actual (4,996) |

| How much does the electricity really cost me if? |||
|---|---|---|
| I.e. How much benefit do I get from the Bonds? |||
| 1 | How many MBCS Bonds do I need? | 10,000 |
| 2 | How much do they cost me in **INR** @ 3 per table? | 3.333 |
| 3 | And what is the Total INR cost of my bill? | 3.333 |
| 4 | *And savings from the existing tariff above? | 1,667 |

| How much does the electricity really cost me if? |||
|---|---|---|
| I.e. How much benefit do I get from the Bonds? |||
| 1 | How many MBCS Bonds do I need? | 10,000 |
| 2 | How much do they cost me in INR @ 4 per table? | 2,500 |
| 3 | And what is the Total Rupee cost of my bill? | 2,500 |
| 4 | *And savings from the existing tariff above? | 2,500 |

| How much does the electricity really cost me? |||
|---|---|---|
| I.e. How much benefit do I get from the Bonds? |||
| 1 | How many MBCS Bonds do I need? | 10,000 |
| 2 | How much do they cost me in Rupees @ 6 per table? | 1,667 |
| 3 | And what is the total Rupee cost of my bill? | 1,667 |
| 4 | *And the savings from the existing tariff above? | 3,333 |

| MBCS Bond table ||
|---|---|
| Bonds purchased | Cost per Bond |
| 1-29,999 | 0.500 |
| 30,000-59,999 | 0.400 |
| 1-29,999 | 0.500 |
| 30,000-59,999 | 0.400 |
| 60,000-99,999 | 0.364 |
| 100,000-149,999 | 0.333 |
| 150,000-199,000 | 0.250 |
| 150,000-199,000 | 0.250 |
| 200,000-249,999 | 0.244 |
| 250,000-299,999 | 0.238 |
| Special Concessionary Rate | 0.167 |

**Figure 6. Electric Bill for Large Consumers in MBCS**

| INDIA Electricity Billing Authority (Reg. Under MBCS) | | | |
|---|---|---|---|
| | Calculations | Costs in INR | Bonds |
| 1 | Units last reading | 4500 | |
| 2 | Units this reading | 4700 | |
| 3 | Units consumed* | 200 | |
| 4 | Artificial price | | 600 |
| 5 | Total subsidized price | | 1,200 |
| 6 | Bonds required | | 1,200 |

| | Bonds |
|---|---|
| Total MBCS Bonds to pay bill | 1,200 |

*Existing electricity tariff cost to consumer (2014)   INR 600   Actual (592)

| How much does the electricity really cost me if? | |
|---|---|
| I.e. How much benefit do I get from the Bonds? | |
| 1 | How many MBCS Bonds do I need? | 1200 |
| 2 | How much do they cost me in INR @ 3 per table? | 400 |
| 3 | And what is the Total INR cost of my bill? | 400 |
| 4 | *And savings from the existing tariff above? | 800 |

| How much does the electricity really cost me if? | |
|---|---|
| I.e. How much benefit do I get from the Bonds? | |
| 1 | How many MBCS Bonds do I need? | 1,200 |
| 2 | How much do they cost me in INR @ 4 per table? | 300 |
| 3 | And what is the Total INR cost of my bill? | 300 |
| 4 | *And savings from the existing tariff above? | 900 |

| How much does the electricity really cost me? | |
|---|---|
| I.e. How much benefit do I get from the Bonds? | |
| 1 | How many MBCS Bonds do I need? | 1200 |
| 2 | How much do they cost me in INR @ 5 per table? | 200 |
| 3 | And what is the total INR cost of my bill? | 200 |
| 4 | *And the savings from the existing tariff above? | 1,000 |

| MBCS Bond table | |
|---|---|
| 1-29,999 | 0.500 |
| 30,000-59,999 | 0.400 |
| 60,000-99,999 | 0.364 |
| 100,000-149,999 | 0.333 |
| 150,000-199,000 | 0.250 |
| 200,000-249,999 | 0.244 |
| 250,000-299,999 | 0.238 |
| 300,000-349,999 | 0.233 |
| 350,000-399,999 | 0.227 |
| 400,000-449,999 | 0.222 |
| 450,000-499,999 | 0.217 |
| 500,00 and above | 0.200 |

**Figure 7. Electric Bill for Medium Consumers in MBCS**

| INDIA Electricity Billing Authority (Reg. Under MBCS) | | | | |
|---|---|---|---|---|
| | Calculations | | Costs in INR | Bonds |
| 1 | Units last reading | 2500 | | |
| 2 | Units this reading | 2600 | | |
| 3 | Units consumed* | 100 | | |
| 4 | Artificial price | | 250 | |
| 5 | Total subsidized price | | | 500 |
| 6 | Bonds required | | | 500 |

| | | Bonds |
|---|---|---|
| Total MBCS Bonds to pay bill | | 500 |
| *Existing electricity tariff cost to consumer (2010) | INR 250 | |

| How much does the electricity really cost me if? | | |
|---|---|---|
| I.e. How much benefit do I get from the Bonds? | | |
| 1 | How many MBCS Bonds do I need? | 500 |
| 2 | How much do they cost me in INR @ 3 per table? | 167 |
| 3 | **And what is the Total INR cost of my bill?** | **167** |
| 4 | *And savings from the existing tariff above? | 83 |

| How much does the electricity really cost me if? | | |
|---|---|---|
| I.e. How much benefit do I get from the Bonds? | | |
| 1 | How many MBCS Bonds do I need? | 500 |
| 2 | How much do they cost me in INR @ 4 per table? | 125 |
| 3 | **And what is the Total INR cost of my bill?** | **125** |
| 4 | *And savings from the existing tariff above? | 125 |

| How much does the electricity really cost me? | | |
|---|---|---|
| I.e. How much benefit do I get from the Bonds? | | |
| 1 | How many MBCS Bonds do I need? | 500 |
| 2 | How much do they cost me in INR @ 6 per table? | 83 |
| 3 | **And what is the total INR cost of my bill?** | **83** |
| 4 | *And the savings from the existing tariff above? | 167 |

| MBCS Bond table | |
|---|---|
| 1-29,999 | 0.500 |
| 30,000-59,999 | 0.400 |
| 60,000-99,999 | 0.364 |
| 100,000-149,999 | 0.333 |
| 150,000-199,000 | 0.250 |
| 200,000-249,999 | 0.244 |
| 250,000-299,999 | 0.238 |
| 300,000-349,999 | 0.233 |
| 350,000-399,999 | 0.227 |
| 400,000-449,999 | 0.222 |
| 450,000-499,999 | 0.217 |
| 500,000 and above | 0.20 |

**Figure 8. Electric Bill for the Small Consumer under MBCS**

## Table 3. Suppose Cost of Petrol in MBCS for 100 gallons
Table 3: Cost of Petrol in MBCS

| Cost of petrol Under MBC System | | | | | | | |
|---|---|---|---|---|---|---|---|
| | | | Rupee Value Price (Current Price) = | 100 | Rupees | | |
| | | | Bond Value Price = | 200 | Bonds | | |
| Typical Purchaser | Quantity (liters) | Rupee Value Price (INR) | Bond Value Price (Bonds) | Four examples of actual cash costs based on number of bonds purchased at one time | | | |
| | | | | 3 | 4 | 5 | 6 |
| Domestic | 1 | 100 | 200 | 66.67 | 50.00 | 40.00 | 33.33 |
| | 10 | 1000 | 2000 | 666.67 | 500.00 | 400.00 | 333.33 |
| | 20 | 2000 | 4000 | 1333.33 | 1000.00 | 800.00 | 666.67 |
| | 40 | 4000 | 8000 | 2,666.67 | 2000.00 | 1600.00 | 1333.33 |
| Small Business | 60 | 6000 | 12000 | 4000.00 | 3000.00 | 2400.00 | 2000.00 |
| | 80 | 8000 | 16000 | 5,333.33 | 4000.00 | 3200.00 | 2666.67 |
| | 100 | 10,000 | 20,000 | 6,666.67 | 5,000.00 | 4000.00 | 3333.33 |
| Larger Business | 200 | 20,000 | 40,000 | 13,333.33 | 10,000 | 8,000 | 6,666.67 |
| | 300 | 30,000 | 60,000 | 20,000.00 | 15,000. | 12,800.00 | 10,000.00 |
| | 400 | 40,000 | 80,000 | 26,666.67 | 20,000. | 16,000.00 | 13,333.33 |

MBSC would offer a special discount to consumers who buy large quantities of bonds at the start of a financial year. A consumer who buys more than INR100, 000 worth of bonds in one transaction in the first month of the year will receive

- 10,000 liters of petrol at INR16 per liter, depending on the prevailing price of petrol per liter,

Or

- any combination of electricity or water or gas at a real price of INR1 per unit up to a limit of 15,000 units or

- Double the above quantities at half the cost of buying the required bonds when settling a bill.

In MBCS, all government-controlled prices (e.g., government fees, post office fees, hospital fees, railway tickets, and airline tickets) will be available by paying twice the number of Bonds as the prevailing price (see 5 for some examples).

Table 4. Example of Economy Class Railway Ticket from Mumbai to Kolkata (INR 640)

|  | Net Price (INR) | Saving (INR) | % |
|---|---|---|---|
| Cost of 1,280 BONDS @ 3 | 427 | 213 | 33.28 |
| Cost of 1,280 Bonds @ 4 | 320 | 320 | 50.00 |
| Cost of 1,280 Bonds @ 5 | 256 | 384 | 60.00 |
| Cost of 1,280 Bonds @ 6 | 214 | 426 | 66.57 |

Note. Prevailing price equals INR640, and price in MBCS equals 1,280 bonds.

### Table 5. Example of an Airline Ticket INR 8,865

|  | Net Price (INR) | Saving (INR) | % |
|---|---|---|---|
| Cost of 17,730 Bonds @ 3 | 5,576 | 3,289 | 32.89 |
| Cost of 17,730 Bonds @ 4 | 4,182 | 4,863 | 46.83 |
| Cost of 17,730 Bonds @ 5 | 3,346 | 5,519 | 55.19 |
| Cost of 17,730 Bonds @ 6 | 2,788 | 6,077 | 60.77 |

**Note:** Airline tickets (with duties and taxes) under present system cost INR 8,865. Under MBCS, a ticket can be purchased using double the amount in Bonds. Number of Bonds required is 8,865 * 2 = 17,730.

All duties will disappear after the system is implemented in total and private businesses will opt for government as a sleeping partner contributing 80 % of liquidity with zero interest but sharing profit and loss in all these businesses in the ratio of 40 to 60 % see the detail under interest free banking.

**The Household Budget and MBCS**

MBCS will deliver real benefits to the basic economic units of consumption: the household and the individual. MBCS enables consumers who plan their expenses to maximize their savings through the calculated use of the marginal Bond cost mechanism. In essence, MBCS encourages purchases in bulk at the start of a financial year. Householders and individuals who are able to assess their needs for the period ahead will be able to accurately decide how many Bonds to purchase.

**The Bond needs of households fall into four basic categories:**

1. Basic consumption needs required to sustain living,
2. Luxury items that bring comfort over and above basic needs,
3. Contingencies that deal with the unexpected in life, and
4. Speculation that covers the desire to profit from the investment of surplus funds.

MBCS Bonds apply to all these situations, and individuals can use the purchase of Bonds to leverage greater value for their money and use the savings to invest.

Table 6 shows a typical middle-class household budget. It should be kept in mind that proposals to include registered businesses in MBCS and the concurrent right of those businesses to import raw materials and finished goods duty free will reduce input costs, transfer prices, and final end-user sales prices.

Table 6. A Typical Middle-class Household Budget

Note. The savings under MBCS are INR79, 379 over pre-MBCS prices, with 24,000 bonds held against the future market at a value of INR5, 581. (Coupons OR Bonds)

| Total Coupon needs | 306,357 |
| Coupon cost in one purchase | 4.3 |

| The Householders Monthly/Annual Budget under the MBCS ||||||||
|---|---|---|---|---|---|---|---|---|
| | Pre MBCS Price | Open Market Trading ||| GOP Priced ||| Total Expenses | Total Coupons |
| | | MBCS Price | 15% Coupons | Total Price | Price | Coupons | Total Price | | |
| **Food, water and clothing** ||||||||||
| Food | 7,280 | 6,500 | 975 | 6,727 | | | | 6,727 | 975 |
| Water | 728 | 650 | 98 | 673 | | | | 673 | 98 |
| Clothing | 7,280 | 6,500 | 975 | 6,727 | | | | 6,727 | 975 |
| **Utilities** ||||||||||
| Gas | 986 | | | | 660 | 880 | 865 | 865 | 880 |
| Electricity | 8,960 | | | | 6,000 | 8,000 | 7,860 | 7,860 | 8,000 |
| Telephone | 5,227 | | | | 3,500 | 4,667 | 4,585 | 4,585 | 4,667 |
| **Other consumables** ||||||||||
| Petrol | 4,107 | | | | 2,750 | 3,667 | 3,603 | 3,603 | 3,667 |
| Diesel | 896 | | | | 600 | 800 | 786 | 786 | 800 |
| Sundry domestic items | 3,500 | 3,045 | 457 | 3,151 | | | - | 3,151 | 457 |
| Auto service/repair | 7,500 | 6,525 | 979 | 6,753 | | | - | 6,753 | 979 |
| Total | 46,463 | 23,220 | 3,483 | 24,030 | 13,510 | 18,013 | 17,699 | 41,729 | 21,496 |
| Total for year | 557,555 | 278,640 | 41,796 | 288,360 | 162,120 | 216,160 | 212,390 | 500,750 | 257,956 |
| **One Off Planned Purchases** ||||||||||
| Radio | 3,500 | 3,045 | 457 | 3,151 | | | - | 3,151 | 457 |
| Fridge | 20,000 | 17,400 | 2,610 | 18,007 | | | - | 18,007 | 2,610 |
| VCR | 25,000 | 21,750 | 3,263 | 22,509 | | | - | 22,509 | 3,263 |
| Gifts | 20,000 | 17,400 | 2,610 | 18,007 | | | - | 18,007 | 2,610 |
| Events | 7,500 | 6,525 | 979 | 6,753 | | | - | 6,753 | 979 |
| Holiday/travel | 35,000 | 30,450 | 4,568 | 31,512 | | | - | 31,512 | 4,568 |
| Total | 111,000 | 96,570 | 14,486 | 99,939 | - | - | - | 99,939 | 14,486 |
| **Contingencies** ||||||||||
| Increased consumption FM | 20,000 | | | - | | | - | - | - |
| Increased consumption GOP | | | | - | 4,500 | 6,000 | 5,895 | 5,895 | 6,000 |
| Unplanned purchases | 15,000 | 13,050 | 1,958 | 13,505 | | | - | 13,505 | 1,958 |
| Unexpecetd events | 10,000 | 8,700 | 1,305 | 9,003 | | | - | 9,003 | 1,305 |
| Estimating | 5,000 | 4,350 | 653 | 4,502 | | | - | 4,502 | 653 |
| Total | 50,000 | 26,100 | 3,915 | 27,010 | 4,500 | 6,000 | 5,895 | 32,906 | 9,915 |
| **Speculative and coupon saving account** ||||||||||
| Hedge against next year | | | 5,000 | 1,163 | | | | 1,163 | 5,000 |
| Save for Wedding | | | 5,000 | 1,163 | | | | 1,163 | 5,000 |
| School Fees | | | 4,000 | 930 | | | | 930 | 4,000 |
| To sell on market/futures | | | 10,000 | 2,326 | | | | 2,326 | 10,000 |
| Total | - | - | 24,000 | 5,581 | - | - | - | 5,581 | 24,000 |
| **Grand Total** | | 718,555 | 401,310 | 84,197 | 420,891 | 166,620 | 222,160 | 218,285 | 639,176 | 306,357 |

## MBCS and the Concept of Marginal Utility

The concept of utility and its relationship to the quantity of any item or service purchased is a cornerstone of microeconomics. Utility is the benefit derived by the buyer from a purchase, and beyond a certain point, the buyer loses the benefit of quantity. This is called marginal utility, and it drives the price people are willing to pay for a good or service. For example, the utility of a glass of water to a man dying of thirst in the desert is very high.

The marginal utility of the next glass of water is also very high. The same cannot be said of a man with ample access to free water.

The same concept applies to the MBCS Bond. It is also different because money and MBCS Bonds do not satisfy needs directly. They are used to exchange for goods and services that have intrinsic value/utility. However, the MBCS Bond has high utility because it can be used for exchange at value.

MBCS Bonds would be purchased to cover a number of useful purposes, and the utility of Bonds can be expressed in savings and speculation. All households and businesses would purchase MBCS Bonds for four basic purposes, depending on means and disposition:

1. They would buy Bonds to save money on planned necessities and luxuries;
2. To provide for unplanned expenditures in the future;
3. To provide room for discretionary expenditures; and
4. To speculate on the price of MBCS Bonds using volume purchases or accumulation.

Table 7 shows how a consumer can use MBCS Bonds.

**Table 7. Consumer's Use of MBCS Bonds**

| Generic Bond Use | Application | Utility or Value | Utility Factor by Income Group | | |
|---|---|---|---|---|---|
| | | | High | Medium | Low |
| Speculative | Store surplus | MBCS Bond purchasers speculate by accumulating surplus Bonds or by buying large discounted quantities to sell at profit | Bond utility is high if the prosperity / attractiveness to speculation is high | Bond utility is high if the prosperity / attractiveness to speculation is high | Bond utility is high if the prosperity / attractiveness to speculation is high |
| | Buy to sell | | | | |
| | Buy to save | | | | |
| | Buy to hoard | | | | |
| | Forward selling | | | | |

| | | | | | |
|---|---|---|---|---|---|
| | Forward buying | | | | |
| Contingencies | Increased basics | Purchasing more MBCS Bonds than planned needs enables discretionary choice in the future. This is of high value when income exceeds the planned expenditure on basics and a few luxuries | High-income consumers will understand the benefit of Bond purchases beyond planned essentials and luxuries | Bond utility becoming marginal beyond contingencies for increased basics and a few more luxuries | Bond utility is marginal at best |
| | More luxuries | | | | |
| | Marriages, births | | | | |
| | Gifts | | | | |
| | Travel | | | | |
| | Rainy days | | | | |
| | Poor estimating | | | | |
| Luxuries | Car | The line between luxuries & basic is very difficult to draw. However, the utility of these items is high for all income groups and is the utility of the MBCS Bonds with which to purchase them | Considered as basic needs by many high income groups and. Therefore, high utility for Bonds | Utility varies by type of goods or service but Bond purchase utility is still high | Bond utility is high once basics are met |
| | TV | | | | |
| | VCR | | | | |
| | White goods | | | | |
| | Computers | | | | |
| | Holidays | | | | |
| Basic Consumption Needs | Electricity | High utility for all basic needs; therefore. Bonds are essential | | | |
| | Water | | | | |
| | Food | | | | |
| | Petrol | | | | |
| | Clothing | | | | |
| | Gas | | | | |

It should also be kept in mind that as the net disposable income of a household increases so does their view of utility. Luxuries become essentials. In other words, as GDP grows, consumers will demand more MBCS Bonds. The cost reductions created by MBCS will enhance savings and investment.

**Why MBCS Bonds Help Businesses**

The MBCS Bond system can help all businesses. In order to participate in MBCS, businesses must register with INMF. All businesses that participate in MBCS are divided into three simple categories, which does away with the myriad of registrations currently in place.

**Category One Business**

A Category one registration does not trade up the value chain in bonds, but it can still purchase MBCS bonds for its ordinary expenses/purchase s. This type of business can register with GMF for Rs.10, 000 or multiples of Rs. 10,000. This fee would entitle the business to Purchase bonds at a special rate of 6 bonds per Rupee throughout the year.

The incentive keeps on increasing with higher amount of registration as shown below in table no 8.

Table 8. Registration Fees for Businesses

| Business Registration Table | | | | | | |
|---|---|---|---|---|---|---|
| With Registration Fee Purchase | | | | Normal Purchase | | |
| Reg. Fee INR | Bonds Collection Entitlement | Entitlement to No. of Bonds to Purchase @ 6 | Amount INR | Amount INR | Rate of Bond | No. of Bond |
| 10,000 | 10,000 | 20,000 | 3,333 | 10,000 | 2.00 | 20,000 |
| 30,000 | 30,000 | 75,000 | 12,500 | 30,000 | 2.50 | 75,000 |
| 60,000 | 60,000 | 165,000 | 27,500 | 60,000 | 2.75 | 165,000 |
| 100,000 | 100,000 | 300,000 | 50,000 | 100,000 | 3.00 | 300,000 |
| 150,000 | 150,000 | 600,000 | 100,000 | 150,000 | 4.00 | 600,000 |
| 200,000 | 200,000 | 820,000 | 136,666 | 200,000 | 4.10 | 820,000 |
| 250,000 | 250,000 | 1,050,000 | 175,000 | 250,000 | 4.20 | 1,050,000 |

| 300,000 | 300,000 | 1,290,000 | 215,000 | 300,000 | 4.30 | 1,290,000 |
|---|---|---|---|---|---|---|
| 400,000 | 400,000 | 1,760,000 | 293,333 | 400,000 | 4.40 | 1,760,000 |
| 450,000 | 450,000 | 2,025,000 | 337,500 | 450,000 | 4.50 | 2,025,000 |
| 500,000 | 500,000 | 2,300,000 | 383,333 | 500,000 | 4.60 | 2,300,000 |
| 550,000 | 550,000 | 2,350,000 | 391,666 | 550,000 | 4.70 | 2,585,000 |
| 600,000 | 600,000 | 2,880,000 | 480,000 | 600,000 | 4.80 | 2,880,000 |
| 700,000 | 700,000 | 3,430,000 | 571,666 | 700,000 | 4.90 | 3,430,000 |
| 800,000 | 800,000 | 4,000,000 | 666,666 | 800,000 | 5.00 | 4,000,000 |
| and above | and above | and above | And above | and above | | and above |

**Note:** These are approximate but incentive based ratios and can be changed according to country's requirement.

**Category Two Business**

A Category two registration passes its goods and services on to an end user (i.e., consumers), and it can register at the start of the year for the upfront sum of Rs. 10,000 or multiple of Rs.10,000. This fee entitles the business to get 20,000 bonds at six bonds per Rupee, provided the business can show that it has collected 10,000 bonds. These bonds could be purchased on the open market or from a customer. The second option is much more business oriented, and therefore, the business would collect more bonds and charge a lower cash price to increase its number of customers. These bonds would be surrendered to INMF in exchange of new bonds without cost. This would eliminate the repeated use of the same bonds by other people or businesses because there would be a record of the issue date. The collection of bonds depends on the registration fee. The more the registration fee, the more the bonds a business can purchase at the rate of 6 bonds per Rupee. This in itself is a cash rebate, and the value depends on the open market exchange rate or the official rate, whichever is better.

**Category Three Business**

A Category Three registration may elect to establish a special relationship with INMF by agreeing to sell its entire output to INMF for surrendering 15% bonds at each sale point. In addition, it would be entitled to import all its capital and other needs into

India duty free at a value equal to what it sells to INMF if the business opts for duty free option and doesn't want bonds. But the registration fee for this category is Rs. **100,000** or multiple of it per year. The combined effect of a supply of bonds up to 15% of the value generated by production and the reduction of costs through the removal of duty on imported items would improve operating margins. Input costs would be substantially reduced, and output prices would stabilize. In addition, these businesses can earn 6 bonds per Rupee if the duty free option is not taken, which would further decrease the costs of inputs as these businesses will not have to spend billions upfront (see the Gold Mine section).

**The Impact of Participating in MBCS**

In MBCS, all three categories of businesses would experience a reduction in the basic costs of doing business. Transforming activity into value for most businesses involves purchasing the following:

1. Capital equipment,
2. Materials and finished items, and
3. Energy.

Each of these items is available to a business under the MBCS scheme. Imported goods are also offered on the same basis, with all tariffs and duties removed once you have the required registration. If this system is strung along the entire chain of business value-added activity, the impact on costs, prices, and margin will be significant.

In MBCS, businesses would have the opportunity to accept cash or cash and Bonds at the point of sale. Their customers and competitors may choose for them because it will be difficult to sell goods and services outside MBCS. Price competition will be too intense.

Businesses will also experience lower operating costs if they participate in MBCS. Travel, telephone calls, petrol, registration fees, stationary, computers, and so forth would be available in MBCS, and the reduced prices available using Bonds would have a significant, positive impact on expenses and overheads.

**Savings for Manufacturers in MBCS**

Table 10 shows the savings available to a Category One business. This Table describes manufacturing costs based on buying Bonds or applying for the duty-free option. The Category 3 registration of INR100,000 would entitle a business to sell merchandise at a maximum of 10 times the registration fee per month or INR12 million worth of goods through INMF in one installment or in, at the most, 12 installments, with each transaction not less than INR1 million. This would reduce the work of INMF to a great extent.

Manufacturers who sell their products through INMF have to deposit 5% in cash or 15% in Bonds of the amount of product sold to INMF. This would entitle a producer to purchase Bonds at the rate of six Bonds per rupee or obtain duty-free imports, depending on the amount sold. The value of the 15% in Bonds would be two and half rupees (if the rate is six Bond per rupee) per INR100. Consumers would happily pay 15% in Bonds because the goods are cheaper as a result of the 50% reduction in production costs. Producers would declare 100% or more of their end products because they want to get back their registration fees by selling extra Bonds at the open-market rate, duty-free goods, or options to other buyers.

Table 10. Analysis of Manufacturing Costs in MBCS

| Cost Class | Activity | MBCS Analysis | | | | | Cash only Price | Non MBCS | MBCS Savings @ 6 | Pre MBCS Prices | Real Cost Savings |
|---|---|---|---|---|---|---|---|---|---|---|---|
| | | Imp. Tariff Price | Cash Outlay | Bonds | Bond cost @ 6 | Total Cash Cost @ 6 | | Artificial Price | | | |
| Capes | Imported Machines | 1,000,000 | 703,704 | 111,111 | 18,519 | 722,222 | 740,741 | * | | 277,778 | 1,000,000 | 259,259 |
| | Local Machines | * | 475,000 | 75,000 | 12,500 | 487,500 | 500,000 | | 12,500 | 550,000 | 50,000 |
| | Imported Equipment | 750,000 | 527,778 | 83,333 | 13,889 | 541,667 | 555,556 | | 208,333 | 750,000 | 194,444 |
| | Local Equipment | | 332,500 | 52,500 | 8,750 | 341,250 | 350,000 | | 8,750 | 385,000 | 35,000 |
| Direct Costs | Imported Materials | 650,000 | 457,407 | 72,222 | 12,037 | 469,444 | 481,481 | | 180,556 | 650,000 | 168,519 |

|  | | | | | | | | | | | |
|---|---|---|---|---|---|---|---|---|---|---|---|
| | Raw Materials | | 218,500 | 34,500 | 5,750 | 224,250 | 230,000 | | 5,750 | 253,000 | 23,000 |
| | Finished Materials | * | 532,000 | 84,000 | 14,000 | 546,000 | 560,000 | | 14,000 | 616,000 | 56,000 |
| | Engineered Items | | 722,000 | 114,000 | 19,000 | 741,000 | 760,000 | * | 19,000 | 836,000 | 76,000 |
| | Consumables | | 53,200 | 8,400 | 1,400 | 54,600 | 56,000 | | 1,400 | 61,600 | 5,600 |
| | Electricity | | 535,714 | 714,286 | 119,048 | 654,762 | | 1,250,000 | 595,238 | 892,857 | 238,095 |
| | Diesel | | 415,714 | 554,286 | 92,381 | 508,095 | | 970,000 | 461,905 | 692,857 | 184,762 |
| Other Costs | Travel | | 636,500 | 100,500 | 16,750 | 653,250 | 670,000 | | 16,750 | 737,000 | 67,000 |
| | Stationary | | 32,300 | 5,100 | 850 | 33,150 | 34,000 | | 850 | 37,400 | 3,400 |
| | Office Equipment | | 121,496 | 19,184 | 3,197 | 124,693 | 127,890 | | 3,197 | 140,679 | 12,789 |
| | Sundry Purchases | | 168,055 | 26,535 | 4,423 | 172,478 | 176,900 | | 4,423 | 194,590 | 17,690 |
| Total | | 2,400,000 | 5,931,868 | 2,054,957 | 342,494 | 6,274,361 | 5,242,568 | 2,220,000 | 1,810,430 | 7,796,983 | 3,612,086 |
| Bonds required under MBCS Scheme | | | | | | | | | | | 2,054,957 |
| Bond Financing @ 10% | | | | | | | | | | | 17,125 |
| Advantage after Financial Charge | | | | | | | | | | | 3,594,961 |
| Saving over Previous Real Costs as a % | | | | | | | | | | | 46.00 |

**Note: Blank boxes indicate that the tariff duty is not available because it changes from time to time.**

Table 10 clearly shows that MBCS would save this company 46% of its costs because it would enjoy duty-free imports and reduced production costs. This analysis is realistic because businesses source inputs from GOI and the open market. The cost of Bonds is assumed to be six Bonds per rupee because the manufacturer requires at least 2 million Bonds. These Bonds can be purchased in one transaction, or they can be purchased during registration with INMF at reduced costs up to the first 1 million Bonds.

### Gold Mine

MBCS will be a gold mine for the Government of India because it would receive at least two and a half percent of the profit from everything produced or sold in the market. The gold from this mine would flow to GOI in the following way:

- A Category 3 business cannot invest the billions of rupees needed to buy cheap Bonds at the beginning of a financial year, so they would sell their products through INMF. This arrangement would entitle the business to buy cheap Bonds or duty-free goods equal to the amount of merchandise sold, and the quota would be 10 times the amount of the registration fee. A registration fee of INR100, 000 would entitle a business to sell INR12 million worth of goods through INMF per year, but it would have to surrender 15% of the amount sold in Bonds to INMF at the time of sale. These Bonds would be returned to GOI, and in return, GOI would allow the business to purchase six Bonds per rupee or obtain duty-free goods and services throughout the year equal to the amount sold through INMF. These Bonds would be resold by GOI, which would keep this profit.

Figure 9. The MBCS Gold Mine

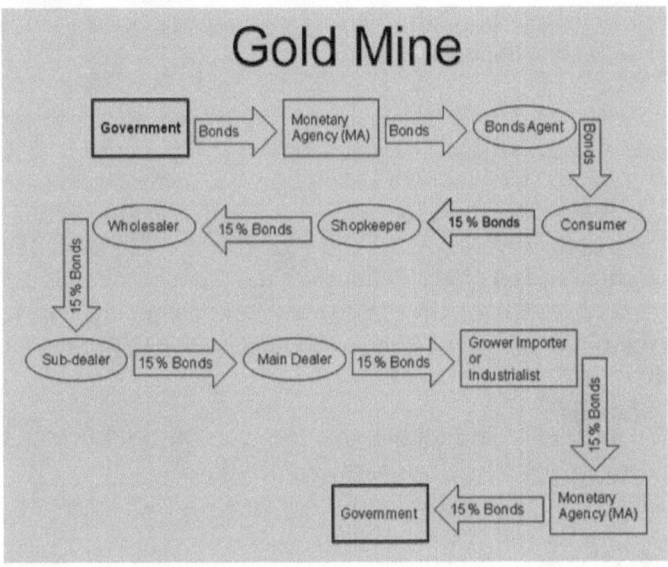

Figure 9 illustrates this gold mine.

**Note: - Suppose if the total daily transactions across India is 100 trillion rupees then by the Gold Mine option the 2.5% of 100 trillion will be 2.5 trillion everyday credited into GOI's account without any compulsion.**

**The Retailer and MBCS**

The benefits of MBCS will cascade down to independent retailers because the use of Bonds and lower prices for manufactured goods will enable retailers to offer consumers lower prices. Retailers will receive special rates for Bonds collected from sales and reduce their costs when purchasing stock. Retailers will have the opportunity to discount prices in MBCS and accept MBCS Bonds in return for discounted with-Bond prices.

The method for calculating retail prices will be different from the method used to determine the prices of GOI-price-controlled goods and services. The actual cost to a retailer is cash plus the cost of the 15% in Bonds. This cost may vary because the actual price paid for Bonds is not fixed.

Bonds collected by a retailer can be traded and used for discounting business-related expenses; therefore, they represent value to a business. In addition, under the rules of MBCS, the collection of Bonds by registered businesses entitles these businesses to buy two to no upper limit (depends on the registration fee) of MBCS Bonds at the rate of six Bonds per rupee. Bonds have tangible value for exchange and trading purposes, and therefore, businesses will be able to account for Bonds in their financial results.

A retailer of a shirt, for example, will calculate price in MBCS based on a number of business considerations:

- Desired operating profit,
- The cost of the shirt,
- Desire for MBCS Bonds, and
- The competitive policy of rivals.

Retailers of shirts, or any other good or service, are unlikely to ignore MBCS because the price of a shirt outside MBCS makes the shirt business unprofitable. Table 11 shows not only the input cost of a shirt, but also the possible sales price if the vendor decides to sell the shirt for cash and Bonds, which is much less than the present price.

**Business Operations and MBCS**

At the end of each year, businesses draw up accounts that demonstrate their business performance in financial terms. In MBCS, accounting for operations will also show how many MBCS Bonds were collected and an assessment of their net worth.

The key question is how does a retailer optimize profits and minimize risk in MBCS. After all, retailers are asked to accept less value prima facie for their goods in MBCS than in the previous system. This question is at the core of MBCS because it applies equally to small, medium, and large businesses, as it does to the Government of India and its agencies.

A rational business has the following objectives:

1. Maximize profits and minimize losses,
2. Maintain a positive cash flow (cash in – cash out = > 0),
3. Recover at least all direct and indirect operating costs,
4. Minimize risk, and
5. Invest cash surpluses in the business.

To achieve these objectives in MBCS, a business will have to:

1. Operate at a level of discount that recovers at least the cash cost of the items for sale, and in this regard, the business can operate separate discount arrangements when the cash costs as a percentage of selling price differ;
2. Use MBCS to buy wholesale goods and services manufactured in India and outside under tax-free and discount import arrangements. This would reduce the cash cost to a business and offer greater scope for deciding discount levels;

3. Use MBCS Bonds to discount all cost inputs, including electricity, travel, stationary, equipment, and so forth;

4. Use discretion when using preferential Bonds (i.e., take account of cash positions and the risk in Bond markets);

5. Use additional Bond facilities to promote growth in business activities/operations; and

6. Accumulate Bonds, as a hedge against future needs only if cheaper sources of Bonds do not exist.

| Retailer Bottom Line Performance Registered MBCS Business | | | | | |
|---|---|---|---|---|---|
| | Discount Scheme Chosen | | | | |
| | 40 | 30 | 20 | 10 | Old System |
| **Cash Revenues** | | | | | |
| MBCS cash sales | 6,000,000 | 7,000,000 | 8,000,000 | 9,000,000 | 10,000,000 |
| Cost of sales | 6,000,000 | 6,000,000 | 6,000,000 | 6,000,000 | 6,000,000 |
| Overhead cost | 200,000 | 2,000,000 | 2,000,000 | 2,000,000 | 2,000,000 |
| Direct cost discounted for coupons @ 15% | 5,700,000 | 5,700,000 | 5,700,000 | 5,700,000 | |
| Overheads reduced by 20% MBCS effect | 1,600,000 | 1,600,000 | 1,600,000 | 1,600,000 | |
| Cost of coupons used @ 6 | 283,333 | 283,333 | 283,333 | 283,333 | |
| Adjusted cost of sales | 7,583,333 | 7,583,333 | 7,583,333 | 7,583,333 | |
| Operating cash profit | (1,583,333) | (583,333) | 416,667 | 1,416,667 | 2,000,000 |
| Finance charges +/- | (158,333) | (58,333) | 41,667 | 141,667 | 200,000 |
| Net profit | (1,741,666) | (641,666) | 458,334 | 1,558,334 | 2,200,000 |
| **Coupons** | | | | | |
| Coupons collected | 8,000,000 | 6,000,000 | 4,000,000 | 2,000,000 | |
| Minimum coupon value @ 6 | 1,333,333 | 1,000,000 | 666,667 | 333,333 | |
| Maximum coupon value @ 2.5 | 3,200,000 | 2,400,000 | 1,600,000 | 800,000 | |
| Median value | 2,266,667 | 1,700,000 | 1,133,333 | 566,667 | |
| Cash & Coupon profit best case | 1,458,334 | 1,758,334 | 2,058,334 | 2,358,334 | |
| Cash & Coupon profit worst case | (408,333) | 358,334 | 1,125,000 | 1,891,667 | |
| Cash & Coupon profit median case | 525,000 | 1,058,334 | 1,591,667 | 2,125,000 | |
| **Optional MBCS Scheme** | | | | | |
| **Additional Coupons** | | | | | |
| Additional coupon entitlement | 24,000,000 | 18,000,000 | 12,000,000 | 6,000,000 | |
| Cost of buying additional coupon | 4,000,000 | 3,000,000 | 2,000,000 | 1,000,000 | |
| Total cash cost of coupons | 4,000,000 | 3,000,000 | 2,000,000 | 1,000,000 | |
| **Total Coupons Held** | | | | | |
| Total collected & purchased | 32,000,000 | 24,000,000 | 16,000,000 | 8,000,000 | |
| Coupons used by business above the line | 1,700,000 | 1,700,000 | 1,700,000 | 1,700,000 | |
| Balance of coupons | 30,300,000 | 22,300,000 | 14,300,000 | 6,300,000 | |
| **Coupon Value** | | | | | |
| Value of coupon held @ 2.5 | 12,120,000 | 8,920,000 | 5,720,000 | 2,520,000 | |
| Value of coupon held @ 6 | 5,050,000 | 3,716,667 | 2,383,333 | 1,050,000 | |
| Median value | 8,585,000 | 6,318,333 | 4,051,667 | 1,785,000 | |
| **Risk Analysis** | | | | | |
| Best outcome | 6,536,667 | 5,336,667 | 4,136,667 | 2,936,667 | 2,200,000 |
| Worst outcome | (533,333) | 133,333 | 800,000 | 1,466,667 | 2,200,000 |
| Median outcome | 3,001,667 | 2,735,000 | 2,468,334 | 2,201,667 | 2,200,000 |
| Best outcome of capital employed % | 56.43 | 50.43 | 43.17 | 34.21 | |
| Worst outcome of capital employed % | (4.60) | 1.26 | 8.35 | 17.09 | 27.50 |
| Median | 25.92 | 25.85 | 25.76 | 25.65 | |
| Risk Analysis | High | Low/Medium | Low | No Risk | High Risk |

Table 12 shows a number of operating scenarios. This Table reveals that business operations can be attractive if additional Bond entitlements are exercised. A business would use these entitlements for future trading and growth. A business' choice of the discount scenario and the related returns/risks is a business judgement that tests the business' appetite for risk, returns, and growth. **Table 12. Impact of MBCS on a Small Retail Business (coupons /bonds)**

Table 12 forecasts and analyzes the impact of MBCS on the operations of a small retail business over the course of a business year. It contains the basic elements of a profit and loss projection together with the number of Bonds collected during the normal course of business under a number of discount scenarios. A risk analysis is also undertaken below the bottom line to determine the impact on profit of holding large amounts of Bonds.

A business must decide business strategies for upcoming years (e.g., pricing policy). In MBCS, a business would have to decide how much risk it is willing to assume in the form of the number of Bonds held/traded. Table 12 shows 40%, 30%, 20%, and 10% discount models, with the balance up to the with-Bond sales price.

In the 40% discount scheme, which means a business accepts 40% of the with-Bond price in MBCS Bonds, a business could double its margin, depending on Bond rates. It could also lose money if the rate for MBCS Bonds falls below five Bonds per INDIA Rupee. A business' margin drops with the drop of Bonds accepted, but so does its risk. A rational businessman would opt for a discount that does not cost money, regardless of the MBCS Bond rate. Risk is reduced considerably after 20%, and margins remain very healthy.

In MBCS, a business would sell many shirt products with different profit margins, which are the critical driver of risk to the enterprise. When margins improve under the scheme, there is more latitude for discounting. This avoids problems associated with cash flow and negative margins. Therefore, a business may choose not to plan its discount across the board but decide on a generic pricing policy of different discounts on different brands and lines, taking account of its cash margin, volume of sales, and the pricing strategies of competitors. In the final analysis, a business would keep an eye on competitors' MBCS pricing policies and how attractive this is to buyers of shirts. This model can be applied to all retail businesses or businesses selling to an end user. It shows how flexible and profitable MBCS can be for well-run businesses.

**Imports and Foreign Exchange Transactions Imports**

The *Hawalla* is one of the key black markets in India, and it denies the government hard currency revenue and real control over foreign exchange. The *Hawalla* is an informal but effective system that enables the flow of currency in and out of India outside the control of the central bank. It is supported by an extensive global network that caters to Indian people's need to buy hard currency in quantity and outside the official system. MBCS can attach itself to foreign currency exchange in and out of India and encourage more money to circulate within the official banking system.

MBCS would offer to buy foreign currency at the official exchange rate and would compete with the *Hawalla* rate by offering extra Bonds over and above the official exchange rate. In the long-term, the MBCS strategy is to do away with any need to compete with the *Hawalla* by making the unofficial market uneconomical. In MBCS, the currency seller would receive a rupee draft equal to the value of the amount of foreign currency at the official exchange rate. In addition, the currency seller would receive 18 Bonds per dollar remitted through official channels, and these Bonds would have a set value in addition to the draft (see Table 13).

Table 13. The MBCS Challenge to the *Hawalla* System

| Foreign currency remittance | Hawalla offers | | Value | MBCS offers official rate and Bonds | | Value in INR-adjusted Bond value | | Benefit over Hawalla in INR per US$* | |
|---|---|---|---|---|---|---|---|---|---|
| US Dollars | INR | Bonds | Bonds | INR | Bonds | Low | High | Low | High |
| 1 | 61 | 0 | 61 | 61 | 18 | 63 | 71 | 2 | 8 |

*The benefit to the user of these extra Bonds will be determined by what he/she does with them. Basic needs would replace

Bonds consumers would have to buy, or they would be cash in hand if they choose to sell their Bonds. For each dollar remitted through official sources, a person would get 18 Bonds free of charge, and the value of these Bonds would vary according to the open-market rate. This is not a devaluation of the rupee, and the government is not charging indirect tax (which is the Bond). The extract value would, therefore, be somewhere in the range of values for MBCS and would depend on the open-market rate of Bonds.

The rate gap would be reversed by offering MBCS Bonds with values that exceed the difference between the official exchange rate and the *Hawalla* rate. This would cause the migration of transactions back into the official exchange rate system. The extent of this migration would be determined, in part, by the value of the credits given in relation to the difference in rupees between the exchange rates. The more Bond points offered, the more attractive the system will appear.

A Bond holder using the exchange rate points system could use Bonds according to MBCS rules. He/she may use them in the dual-price scheme without having to pay cash for the Bond points. He/she could also use a Bond account transferable to anybody in India or sold openly on the market for rupees.

The Bond does not constitute cash; therefore, the government is not matching the *Hawalla* rate in rupees but merely offering to reduce taxes through the subsidized price system. The person making the transaction could use the Bond value against any purchase in the mutual benefit Bond system. Therefore, the additional Bond points may be used to purchase consumer goods or utilities at the Bond price.

The *Hawalla* exists because the government protects the national interest by setting nonmarket rates and denying people the right to hold foreign currency in their own personal accounts. In the long-term, MBCS would render this policy redundant and make all smuggling economically unattractive or redundant.

Rough estimates show that if only 20% of India's population spends INR100, 000 within 24 hours the government would collect INR 24 trillion, which is much more than the INR 17.9 trillion needed by the government. With the MBCS scheme, the government would collect more than 10 years worth of budgets in 30 days, and the gold mine option would generate 100 times more than the annual budget.

## A MACROECONOMIC CASE FOR MBCS

MBCS would generate much more revenue for the Government of India than the present revenue system. In addition, MBCS would resolve the systemic crisis that is causing India's entire economy to seriously under perform.

The macroeconomic impact of MBCS focuses on a number of economic drivers that result in the output of the economy expressed as Gross Domestic Product (GDP). The impact of MBCS at a macro level focuses on the economic system in India that supports GDP. This is the way that capital and finance, trade and manufacturing, agriculture and services, tax policy and tax systems, human resources (including employment), national infrastructure, interest rates, imports and exports, and so forth operate together to produce wealth.

### What is Wrong with the Current Economic System in India?

The indirect tax system causes the largest problem for India's economy. This system may threaten to sink the ship of state in an ocean of debt in the near future although not at present. In addition, this malfunctioning system has a negative effect on all other systems. For example stable exchange rates, investment in people and industry, low-cost financing, and so forth are not possible because the direct and indirect tax system is the main obstacle. This reinforces economic failure, and beyond a certain point, it can cause the economy to collapse.

The failure of Govt. to collect enough revenue through taxation is the result of a failed tax system, and it has forced the government to use their own resources in large amounts of money in order to finance regular government deficits. The vast majority of this expense is the barrowed money with interest. Again, when a major part of an economic system starts to fail, then the entire system's performance is in jeopardy.

Figure 10 illustrates the fragile state of India's economic system and why it is under performing. As with all macroeconomics, it is a complex system that requires skills at the highest level to manage. This is usually the job of government. However, at the grassroots level of any economic system is the investor: the person, corporate body, group of investors, institutions, pension funds, and so forth who decide to defer expenditure/dividends in favor of investment. In India, the investor is faced with obstacles if he/she wishes to create wealth through investment because of low returns, high risks, import duties, high commodity prices, and, most significant, high direct and indirect taxes. No economy in this basic condition can hope to develop long-term strength and growth.

### Figure 10. Fragile State of India's Economy

The system of economic realities in India

India's problems are about 'system failure'

- Low government revenues
- Burdensome taxes
- External borrowing with

High levels of national debt (e.g. to finance defense!)

Large external interest based debt repayments

Public Debt
Rs 45, 80,472 crore
67.7 % of GDP(2014)

External Debt
$440 billion (2014)

Tax burdens causes evasion and create a black economy

No surplus GOI revenue to spend on vital infrastructure

PC GDP of $3,800 (PPP)

GOI
Revenue: $198 billion
Expenditure: $292 billion

## The Way Out of the Crisis

In times of crisis, it is sometimes difficult to see the issues clearly because crisis management shortens and narrows people's vision. In the case of India, and other developing countries, it is difficult to look beyond the current system and the way taxes are collected. However, if a solution is to be found, then it must be outside the current tax system. As stated elsewhere and as is generally accepted among experts and the general public, I India's current tax system does not work and, more important, is unlikely to meet future needs.

MBCS would meet not only the short-term needs of India; it would also provide a system that creates wealth and prosperity for a large proportion of India's population. In short, MBCS would produce four first-order results immediately:

1. Collect more than INR50 Trillion in first 30 days of operation and at least 100 times more by the end of fiscal year; and

2. Enable Govt. to achieve short-, medium-, and long-term solvency (i.e., India would be able to balance its budget, avoid external debt, and invest in the country's future). Figure 11 illustrates how MBCS would improve India's economy.

Massive sales of MBCS Shares in Q1 will transform Government Finances
- Improve liquidity from normal tax collection drag
- No short term cash deficit borrowing
- Facilitate budget surplus
- Remove rolling budget deficits
- Repay external debts

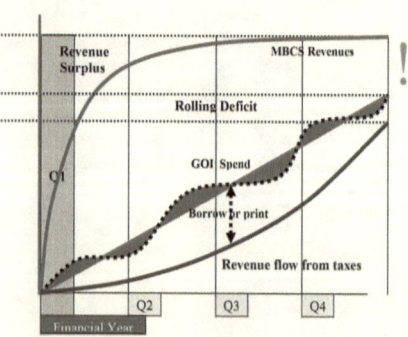

MBCS would produce a properly functioning economic system characterized by:

1. Balanced budgets,
2. Improved confidence in the system,
3. Investment in the infrastructure, and
4. Continuous economic growth.

## How MBCS Produces a Properly Functioning Economic System

**MBCS works on the principle that**

- The Government of India will discount its current prices for controlled goods and services in order to obtain upfront funds and lower input costs, which will promote the growth of GDP;
- MBCS will transfer value from imports and supplies of goods and services to manufacturing units to the core added-value activities in agriculture, manufacturing, retail, and services;
- MBCS will attract money from the black market because the new MBCS pricing levels will compete with it for customers, and because MBCS provides for speculation, black money will be used to purchase Bonds for trade; and
- The *Hawalla* system will become less attractive because MBCS Bonds will bridge the gap between official and unofficial foreign exchange rates.

MBCS will produce four first-order (i.e., short-term) results:

1. GOI solvency and improved gross revenues.
2. Improved profitability of all businesses.
3. Reduced black market operations.
4. Increased foreign currency holdings.

**MBCS will produce four second-order (i.e., medium-term) results:**

1. Net surpluses for GOI and, therefore, more GOI investment.
2. Cash surpluses for Indian businesses, which will encourage investment.
3. Eliminate hoarding and increased money liquidity.
4. Reduce foreign debt and eliminate official and unofficial exchange rates.

**MBCS will produce four third order (i.e., long-term) results:**

1. Increased national human productivity and health and reduced levels of poverty.
2. Increased private investment and the growth of GDP until it sustains acceptable standards of living for all citizens.
3. A free-market economy with few internal/external barriers and tax burdens and a general awareness that government solvency is critical for maintaining the security, welfare, and prosperity of the system and the people of India.
4. The ability of GOI and the central bank to plan for future foreign exchange needs, which will stabilize the rupee.

These results depend on the ability of MBCS to deliver significantly more cash to GOI than the current tax system.

MBCS will provide the largest contribution to the revenue system when this system is applied to all economic transactions in India's economy. Economic activity usually involves a string of supporting importers, material and equipment suppliers, and service companies that form a chain to the manufacturer or provider of goods and services. This activity is also supported downstream by logistics and wholesale distributors. This system is often referred to as the value-added chain because it shows how the value/eventual price of a product or service is built up at each stage.

MBCS, through INMF, would offer to buy the total output from agriculture, manufacturing, and certain services from producers at agreed prices plus 5% in cash or 15% in Bonds. People would be encouraged to participate in MBCS because they would be able to take advantage of the duty-free importation of capital, material, and goods.

To estimate the impact of MBCS, a simple model has been developed based on existing data concerning India's GDP and how it is broken down. The model assumes that at the first stage of value addition there are activities by importers and suppliers. Thereafter, the core added-value sectors of agriculture, industry, and services are included, followed by distribution.

The model is simplified because the supply chain of some manufacturing and service businesses can be complex. For example, equipment suppliers have a sub chain and distributors who supply factories and offices. Although this chain can be complex, MBCS would produce more revenue as the number of Bond transactions increase.

### Sustaining the Value of the MBCS Bond

The MBCS Bond is intended to have negotiable value throughout its life. While the cost of a Bond is determined by the price paid for it, an unused Bond also has an open-market value because of the demand for goods and services.

The maintenance of value is critical because it is likely that Bond value will fluctuate within reasonable limits. This will encourage people to save Bonds in the same way they save shares, savings certificates, and gold and silver.

The MBCS Bond would be subject to the following:

1. It would be subject to substantial, continual demand because of the need to sustain economic activity.

2. It would be subject to the maintenance of supply management controls to ensure Bonds sustain GDP growth without the danger of inflation.

3. Open-market operations through INMF agents and private sellers would ensure that buyers/sellers/agents would act in their best interests to maintain a stable, positive market rate.

4. The limited period of cheaper Bonds at the beginning of a financial year will ensure a healthy open market when official channels dry up or become relatively expensive. This alone will keep minimum open-market rates above or around five Bonds per Rupee.

5. It is anticipated that banks and finance houses will purchase large quantities of Bonds at the start of each year and hold them for their customers. As a result, a bank's customers would be able to purchase Bonds at any time during the year and in large quantities provided they are willing to pay the bank's risk and profit margin.

**The Government of India's MBCS Balance Sheet and Cash Flow**

MBCS will produce revenues in the following areas:

1. The sale of Govt. price-controlled goods and services.
2. Operations in India's added-value chain.
3. The use of MBCS Bonds in the retail sector.
4. The use of MBCS as an import agency for goods and services arriving in India for sale or use in the country.

Table 15 and Figure 12 show how MBCS produces revenues. In some cases, these figures are estimates based on broad economic data, and as such, they are no better and no worse than methods deployed by governments to forecast tax revenues.

It is important to remember that the concession made by Govt. to start MBCS (i.e., reducing the price of controlled items) is more than compensated for by:

1. Reduced Black money (i.e., its migration to the open, lawful economy) and
2. Increased India's GDP.
3. Table 15. The State of GOI's Finances in MBCS

| Total receipts in billions Rupees | | | | | | |
|---|---|---|---|---|---|---|
| Revenue Stream | Years from MBCS Introduction | | | | | |
| | 1 | 2 | 3 | 4 | 5 | Average |
| GOI-controlled goods and services | 5000.00 | 6000.0 | 7200.0 | 8640.0 | 10360.8 | 7440.1 |
| Receipts from retail markets | 1500.00 | 1800.0 | 2160.0 | 2590.2 | 3110.0 | 22300.2 |
| Receipts from industry and commerce | 9140.25 | 10970.1 | 13160.5 | 15790.8 | 18950.8 | 136000.7 |
| Total receipts from current activity | 15640.25 | 18770.01 | 22520.52 | 27030.02 | 32430.63 | 232800.1 |
| Beneficial receipts from exchange control | 1200.00 | 1200.00 | 1200.00 | 1200.00 | 1200.00 | 12000.00 |
| Grand Total | 16840.25 | 19970.10 | 23720.52 | 28230.02 | 33630.63 | 24480.1 |
| Absorption of black economy % | 200 | 200 | 200 | 200 | 200 | 200.00 |
| GDP Growth Forecasts | 80 | 100 | 120 | 120 | 130 | 110.00 |

**Note:** This Table does not include the funds and benefits that would result from the Gold Mine, unused money, interest free banking, corporate farming, or foreign investment.

Above are all approximate figures as the exact amount can't be determined till the system is actually implemented for a whole period of at-least 1 year.

### Corporate Farming

In MBCS, Govt. would provide selected corporate farming organizations with up-to-date machinery and equipment, free water, low-cost electricity, and low-cost fuel. Airplanes would be used to spray pesticides and sow seeds. Boundaries would vanish except on paper and in computers, and land could be sold without fear of litigation. The government would share profits with these corporations, which would reduce the subsidies presently paid out by Govt. As a result, every piece of land would be cultivated with high-quality crops and at the cheapest production costs. Govt. would export these crops and earn much-needed foreign exchange and use corporate farming agencies to sell these crops inside the country. Therefore, the government would be able to easily regulate the price of these crops.

**The True Interest Free Banking System**

This system serves the same purpose as conventional banking, but it is based on the idea of profit and loss sharing. The Interest free banking system is guided by the concepts of *profit sharing, safekeeping, joint venture, cost plus, leasing*.

In order to avoid charging or paying interest in a mortgage transaction, the interest free banking system uses an approach called *Cost Plus*. A bank may buy a house and sell it to a prospective buyer at a profit or build a house on turnkey basis. The buyer pays for the house in installments. These installments are the actual loan plus rent, which is a percentage of the prevailing interest rate and which is reduced with every installment. A bank may also use an approach called *leasing*. In this approach, a bank will sell a vehicle to a buyer in exactly the same way as it will sell a house. The bank's profit is from the rent of the house or car, not from selling it at a higher price to the buyer. This is true interest free banking.

In the *Joint venture* approach, a company repays a bank loan by sharing its profits with the bank. This profit-sharing agreement ends when the loan is repaid.

Using the *profit sharing* approach, a bank and borrower enter into a joint venture. The bank provides venture capital, and the borrower provides the labor. In this way, the bank and borrower share the risk and the profit.

**The true form of interest free banking is *partnership* (i.e., sharing, profit and loss), and this will constitute about 90%**

to 95% of the major business carried out in MBCS. *Leasing* will form the basis for the final 5% to 10% of transactions. Once MBCS is implemented, there will be a massive transfer of funds from private accounts. As a result, private banks will depend on government funds to provide money to businesses and industries. Figure 13 illustrates how interest free banking will work in MBCS.

### Figure 13. How Interest free Banking works in MBCS

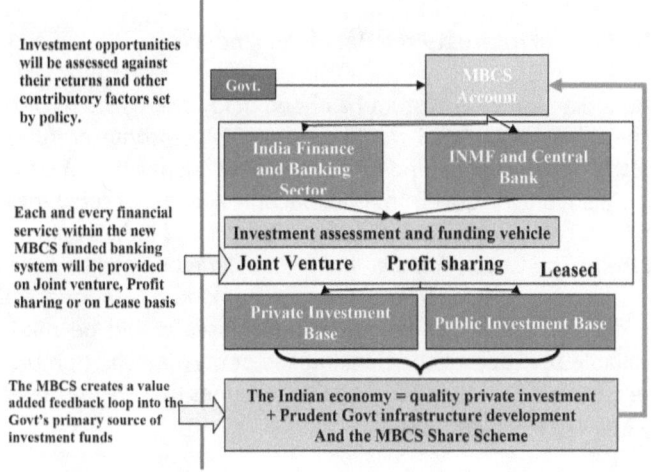

### Figure 14. India's Economic Recovery under MBCS

The key factor for success is Interest free banks' relationship with the depositor. Interest free banking must develop attractive low-, medium- and high-risk investment products. It must issue credit cards in order to compete with other banking systems. In addition, interest free banking must develop acceptable short- and medium-term cash flow financing management facilities for businesses and individuals. In short, interest free banks must become credible, respected go-betweens that link investment with opportunity.

Although interest free banks must develop customer services that can compete with interest-based banks, customers also need to become responsible investors. People must be prudent and develop realistic expectations. They must become aware that they have a responsibility to the wider community when they invest. Prudent, responsible investment will help alleviate poverty and ease the burden on people who support the poor. Banks do not own a depositor's money; they just manage it. Therefore, consumers must demand change before there is a shift from interest-based banking to true interest free banking.

**The Start of Interest-Free Banking in India**

The Indian banking system has been held back by the lack of official liquidity. MBCS would change this by producing funds for the Government of India The stronger cash position of Govt. would enable the government to become a lender of substance, and this can be used to determine the nature of India's banking system. The Government of India could lend on condition that its loans support only interest free banking operations and products. In short, massive cash surpluses would be made available by Govt. to the banking sector on the condition that the money would be used to finance schemes that are approved by appropriate committees.

MBCS would promote interest-free banking because it will reduce the risk of project failure and enable bankers to make more accurate forecasts about project revenues and profits.

Figure 15 illustrates the role of banks in MBCS.

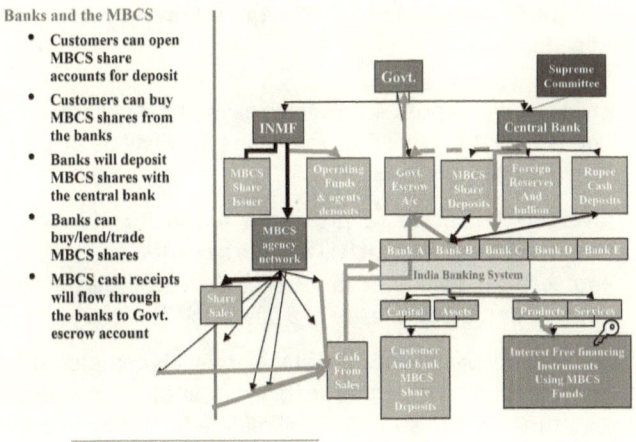

Creating an incentive based economy

## Figure 15. Role of Banks in MBCS
### Interest-Free Banking

Interest-free banking seems to be impossible because interest has very deep, firm roots in the global marketplace; however, if MBCS totally replaces current tax systems, interest-free banking becomes a real possibility. Once MBCS is fully implemented, money belonging to the private sector held by banks will be transferred to Indian Government accounts. Once there are few funds available to banks from the private sector, they will have to depend on Govt., which will be more than willing to provide funds, but only on a profit-and-loss sharing basis. Banks will have no option but to take loans from Govt. and invest in the private sector on the same basis, but only after making sure the investment is profitable. Any bank constantly losing money will not be given fresh loans and face being closed down. In MBCS, banks will profit from the hundreds of new businesses and industries that would be created by a dynamic, growing economy.

**Role of the Central Bank**

Under MBCS, banks would follow the following rules when providing loans:

1. Investors will deposit a 20% down payment as collateral and deposit it in the bank. The remaining 80% will be provided by the state.
2. Investors will have to provide a feasibility study of a proposed project, and it will have to be verified by the bank and certified by the central bank. Govt. will be the final authority on the feasibility of a business or industry.
3. No cash will be advanced until the project is completed but only the running expenses are given from the 20% deposits (i.e., turn-key basis). This will eliminate the major cause of bad debts.
4. Operating expenses will be paid from the 20% down payment received by the bank. In some cases, the investor may have to put down more than 20% in order to cover operating costs.
5. No other collateral is needed.
6. Bank will employ a team of experts on a commission basis, and they will be paid from the profit according to a pre-agreed contract. In case of loss, the team of experts will not receive any commission. Any team repeatedly incurring losses will be blacklisted and will not be able to obtain new contracts. This condition will safeguard the bank from major losses.
7. Any bank constantly showing losses will not be awarded fresh loans and faces going out of business, so the chances of bad loan or losses are completely eliminated.
8. The state will not interfere with any business sponsored by it, but the central bank can and will interfere in the case of loss or fraud.
9. The share of the profit will be 40/60, where sate will accept 40%, and the remaining 60% will be divided between the

investor and the bank when the bank is a partner with an investor.

10. Investors or a bank can increase their investment up to 60%, and 40% will be invested by the state. In these cases, the profit margin will be 80/20. The state will receive 20%, and the bank and investors will divide the remaining 80%.

11. The distribution of profits between investors and a bank is an internal affair and will not be influenced by the state, but the final contract between the investor and bank will part of the main contract.

12. The state will provide duty-free raw material, machinery and other equipment, electricity, telephone service, fuel, and other services below cost. This will increase the profitability of businesses as the production cost for them is reduced. The state will cover the loss incurred by providing below-cost services and recover it from the profit. It is expected that the net income of the state will never be less than 20%, even after providing below-cost services. This incentive will only be given to big businesses, and because the government will be a shareholder in all these businesses, it will realize trillions of Rupees in profit every year.

**MBCS banking will have some profound effects on the economy:**

1. Bankruptcy laws will be eliminated and end the unchecked profit of liquidators, which cause tremendous loss to shareholders and investors. The courts will deal with rare cases of fraud.

2. The state will establish interest free insurance and ensure that the investor is protected from an unexpected loss in case of fire or natural calamities. To insure this loss, the investor has to deposit 5% of the profit in a government account for a time period decided by the investor. If there is no catastrophic event, the state will refund the investor's money minus the profit the state has earned from it. The investor is secured, and the loss is covered by state. With all these checks and balances, the chances of major loss

are less than 0.1%, which can be covered by the profits the government earns from the investors who participate in this insurance scheme.

The central bank will play an important role in the MBCS banking system. Its experts will check every feasibility study before allowing a bank to go ahead with an investment.

**Impact of MBCS on India's Banks**

Interest-free banking will increase banks' profits because hundreds of new businesses and industries will take advantage of the large amount of money available with a 20% down payment as collateral. Banks will also make profits by buying and selling Bonds to their Bond account holders. Interest-based banking will be eliminated because there will be no money available to invest. Even if money was available, it would be impossible to attract people willing to borrow money on an interest basis.

In MBCS, consumers would have only one account, and this account would earn profit on a daily basis. This profit will not be based on interest; instead, consumers will earn profit on a profit-and-loss sharing basis. Consumers would be able to open a government account or a bank account, and this will be guided by the best rate of return.

Credit cards would be available to consumers, but their spending limit would be restricted to the amount of money they have in a bank account. Every month the profit would be calculated according to the deposits remaining in that account. This will solve the problem of overspending, which is a prevalent problem in developed countries.

**IMPLEMENTING MBCS**

**The Government of India's Role in MBCS**

MBCS requires the wholehearted endorsement of the Government of India, and people must recognize its role as the sponsor of MBCS. Laws must be put in place to establish MBCS and a system for distributing Bonds, collecting revenue, and overseeing and administering the scheme. The government would also play a key role in setting policy.

Each year, the Finance Ministry would determine the total Bond value and the denominations and terms and conditions for Bond use, and it would take into account the number of Bonds already in circulation. The Bonds would have a face value representing Rupees, and it would be necessary to exercise monetary controls to prevent inflation and keep the supply within reasonable limits that neither hinder activity nor cause a reduction in a Bond's face value. This is already a common part of fiscal policy.

In essence, the government would authorize the issue of Bonds at a value approximating the needs of the state budget and the anticipated level of economic activity. As prediction is an art and not a science, budget surpluses and deficits arising from windfalls and shortfalls would have to be managed in the medium- to long-term (i.e., through the next year's budget or through emergency mid-term budgets). The government would have to control MBCS policy and strategy because it is a state revenue system. It would also need to ensure that MBCS remains relevant in concept, objectives, and implementation.

The following criteria will ensure the ongoing success of MBCS:

1. MBCS must be accessible in all parts of the country and for US expatriates abroad.
2. It is necessary for the system to continually make goods and services available at realistic prices.
3. There must be real discounts for using Bonds.

If these issues are always addressed, the system will take care of itself because demand for Bonds will always exist.

**The Implementation Strategy**

The following is not intended as an exhaustive description of implementing the system. Instead, only the basic features of implementation are discussed.

Prior to the launch of the scheme, the Government of India must tender contracts that cover the following tasks essential to the launch and administration of MBCS:

1. A general management and administration contract.
2. A card/Bond design, security, and manufacturing contract.
3. An audit contract.

These contracts will form the structure for MBCS in India

There are certain activities that must be performed in order to make the scheme a success:

o Publicizing and marketing the system throughout India
o Setting up the Bond infrastructure (i.e., logistics) so the card/Bond system is available throughout the marketing area.
o Printing and manufacturing Bonds.
o Entering into contracts with Bond vendors.
o Gathering, consolidating, controlling, and accounting for the revenue received from the sale of MBCS card/Bonds.

It will be necessary to simplify the administration and revenue-gathering functions in order to ensure MBCS is a success. Therefore, it may be best to assign all of the roles set out above to one particular organization. However, there are also benefits to awarding the above contracts to different, competent organizations in India.

It is assumed that a major Indian bank(s) can play management/administrative roles in the nationwide structure gathering revenues from card/Bond sales and consolidating them into a national interest account made available to the government. A bank that administers MBCS will be given a percentage of the net proceeds. This involves no cash outlay by the government.

It may be considered prudent to hand the administration of the Bond system to the same bank, provided it has a network of branches with access to the anticipated source of revenues. This will ease administration costs and enhance accountability.

In order to make Bonds available to the largest number of people, it will be necessary to recruit Bond vendors. In order to cover the entire population of India, it may be necessary to employ as many as 50 to 100 million Bond vendors in cities, towns, and, in some cases, villages. This would improve the employment situation among the many educated Indians who are currently unemployed.

Each Bond agent will be employed on 10% commission bases, so INR100 worth of Bonds will be sold for INR90. These agents will be registered with INMF and pay INR5000 a year, which will be used by INMF to establish a network of offices and modern communications throughout the country. It is estimated that at least 100,000 offices will be needed to serve the Bond agents. Each Bond agent will be required to sell INR300, 000 a month and this can be increased according to demand. An agent who cannot pay the INR5000 fee will be required to sell INR150, 000 until he/she is able to pay the registration fee.

## Incentive for Multiplication Effect to Investor, Govt. & Poor Population.

Investors who purchase INR100, 000 worth of Bonds to sell to people who cannot purchase large quantities of Bonds during the discount period (i.e., six Bonds per rupee during the first month of a financial year) would be able to negotiate a 5% to 7% discount from the Bond seller, who would pay this out of his or her 10% commission. The Bond seller would be willing to give an investor this discount because the investor would need to purchase large quantities of Bonds during the discount period. In this scheme, the investor would sell Bonds at the discount rate and keep the 5% to 7% negotiated with the Bond seller as profit. As a result, instead of only 5% of the population being able to take advantage of the discount period, at least 50% of the population would be able to take advantage of the low rates available during the discount period. Not only would this benefit large numbers of average people, it would also provide GOI with more money.

**By the end of 30 days of discount period the investor has earned 50%-150% profit depending on his efforts to resell the Bonds at Government rates but keeping the share of his profit of 5%-7% which he has negotiated with the Bond agent. This will be an open secret and even a non investor will join in this Mega Sale by Hook or Crook (Borrowing from Banks, selling valuables like Gold) or forming teams to collect 100,000 required.**

**Multiplication Effect to Investor, Govt. & Poor Population**

**Grassroots Organization**

Bond vendors will retain a percentage of all sales. This will be their only form of payment. It is incentive based and promotes far more activity than a government salary.

The use of references, educational requirements (e.g., minimum O level standard), and some form of collateral guarantees will ensure competent people become vendors. Cash deposits may be deemed suitable under the circumstances. Most vendors will be students or unemployed people.

Simplicity is the key to success, but it may be necessary to establish a supervisory level because of the number of card/Bond vendors involved in selling MBCS Bonds. This supervisory layer should be kept to a minimum so the effectiveness of the card/Bond system is not affected and to prevent abuse. Using an existing bank structure/organization appears to be the most logical and expedient method for creating an instant administrative framework. (See Figure 16 for details about the structure of MBCS in India)

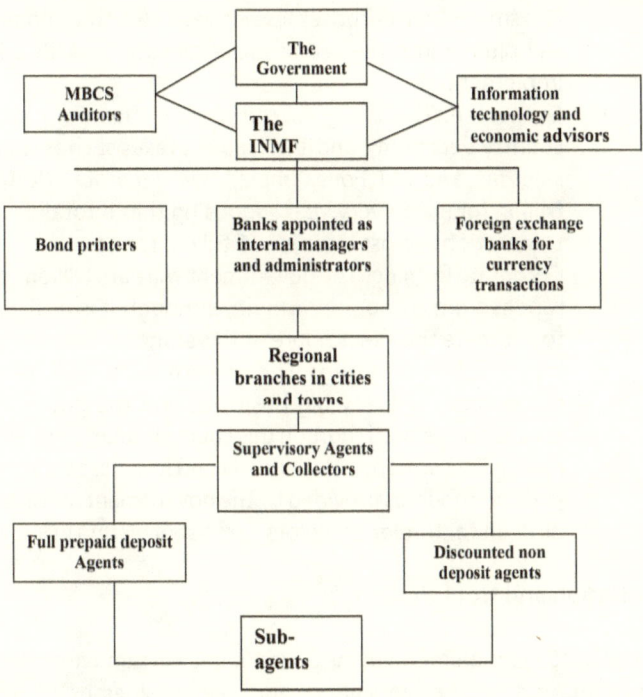

**Figure 16. The Proposed Structure of MBCS in India**

**A Flood of Money**

As mentioned earlier, there is a flood of money waiting to wash into government accounts. This money will come from a number of sources:

- Massive sale of Bonds: It is expected that within one month 20% of the population will buy INR24 trillion worth of Bonds, and its multiplication effect will

generate another INR36 trillion because at least 50% of the population will join in this massive incentive scheme.
- Black money: According to very conservative estimates, approximately US$100 trillion is being used for smuggling purposes every year. All this money will plunge into the sea of profit as soon as MBCS is implemented.
- Gold mine: This is considered the backbone of every country's economy, and it will replace taxes such as GST, sales tax, and VAT. For example, it will generate INR900 trillion for India every year supposing that if total daily transactions across India is 100 trillion rupees.
- Corporate farming. The government will earn trillions of rupees from corporate farming, although it is difficult to estimate the exact figure at this stage.
- Interest free banking: The government will be a shareholder in every big business, and the potential revenue generated through this source is unimaginable.
- foreign investments: With no tax and low-cost services and commodities provided by the government, it will be difficult for foreign investors to resist investing in India.

**Deflation and Not Inflation**

Once MBCS is implemented, the government will remove control on all imports, exports, agriculture, and major businesses but will act as a partner. This will eliminate the control of these economic areas by cartels. This will help stop inflation because MBCS will eliminate the price hikes cartels use to improve profits. Without these price hikes, there will be no inflation. Although inflation will be eliminated in MBCS, there is a possibility of deflation. This possibility will exist as long as the government remains true to the incentives that drive MBCS.

**Interest Free Bonds Instead of all Other Interest Based Financial Instruments**

The following criteria must be used to float interest free bonds (i.e., MBCS Bonds):

1. No interest will be paid on these bonds (i.e., Bonds).
2. They will not increase the debt burden of the government and should not require any guarantee to print them.
3. Bonds must be available on a supply and demand basis at all times and have no restriction on the amount.
4. Bonds must benefit everybody when used with real currency to purchase goods and services.
5. Bonds cannot be hoarded and should be available from different sources; however, the rate may differ from day to day and from place to place.
6. Everybody must have the opportunity to buy bonds at the cheapest rate.
7. Buying and selling bonds must occur like any other commodity, but unlike other commodities, these will never be in short supply.
8. Bonds must have an unlimited shelf life.
9. Daily, weekly, or monthly inter bank rates must be based on actual currency but without interest.
10. Bonds must be available to registered businesses at the cheapest rate throughout the year.
11. People must be able to buy bonds 24 hours a day, 365 days a year.
12. People must be able to buy unlimited amounts of bonds.

MBCS will result in the following benefits for India and its people:

1. Because of the strong profit incentive, the government will sell bonds worth LBP trillions every year, and there will be

massive revenue collection by the government early in the fiscal year and throughout the year.

2. There will be a strong incentive to buy bonds using foreign currency, which will result in large hard currency reserves.
3. There will be daily lotteries to provide average citizens with a chance to share in the profits earned by the government.
4. There will be no kickbacks as is the case in the sale of international bonds, which only benefit a few highly placed people.
5. Black money will be used to purchase these bonds. This flood of black money will enable the government to invest in big projects, such as dams to produce electricity and oil/gas field and mineral exploration.
6. All spare and unused money or valuables will be used to buy these bonds for business purposes and reduce the cost of all types of bills and commodities.
7. These bonds will reduce costs at least 10% to 20% from the present price and at least 50% when these bonds are bought at the cheapest rate.
8. The sale of these bonds will provide job opportunities for millions of unemployed, educated people.
9. Bonds can be treated just like money and will be available in the form of debit cards.
10. Even the poorest person should be able to buy and sell bonds **at** a prompt margin.

India has been used as an example of MBCS because the country is at a crossroads. What is undertaken in the next 3 to 5 years will have a profound effect on the long-term political stability and financial security of India and its international prestige. The improvement of the Government of India's liquidity is vital to India's political stability and financial security. India cannot afford more budget deficits. Current levels of Govt. indebtedness require a regular restructuring of external debt as well as massive interest payments.

Many Indian people believe there is fixed or diminishing wealth in India the people and government appear to be fighting against this vanishing wealth, and taxation is their battleground. This idea is flawed and dangerous because it fails to see the promise of growth held by a solvent government able to build roads, schools, hospitals, ports, airports, and other infrastructure projects, which would inject vital value into the economy and increase the GDP of India in other words, a solvent government will produce a bigger cake for everyone to share.

MBCS provides India with the opportunity to work its way out of the downward spiral of diminishing value and diminishing tax revenues. By improving the government's ability to collect revenue and spend it wisely, the country's economy can move in a positive direction. In addition, MBCS revenue would increase the growth in GDP. The country could once again pay its way in the world without the need for foreign loans. It is necessary to reverse India's downward economic and political spiral and fulfill the expectations of its citizens.

MBCS is a government revenue system that has a wide range of applications to national economies. It is not solely a system for helping developing economies and poorer countries. It can also be used by developed and advanced economies. Indeed, in the fast-growing global marketplace, today's economic giants are being challenged by the Asian tigers, and in order for them to compete; they need to respond in an innovative and responsible way. No economy can rest too comfortably on its past economic performance or its assumptions about the future. In fact, in the new global marketplace, governments need to rethink how they collect and use revenue.

According to Michael Porter of the Harvard University Business School, national economies can be classified using the following four basic characteristics:

1. factor driven,
2. diversified production base,

3. research and development, and
4. Wealth driven.

These characteristics show the path from dependence on extraction industries to the achievement of wealth using investments. Of course, all four conditions can co-exist in any economy; however, Porter suggests that an economy's stage of development can be determined by identifying which characteristic dominates an economy.

It is also possible to identify a nation's stage of economic development by examining its citizens' quality of life. The United Nations uses the Human Development Index (HDI) to measure the quality of life in each country. Although HDI uses a broad range of measures, economics is a core measure because the richest nations tend to have the highest HDI scores.

Table 16 shows some sample HDI scores.

| HDI Rank | Country | Human development index (HDI) value 2014 |
|---|---|---|
| 1 | Norway | 0.955 |
| 2 | Iceland | 0.906 |
| 3 | Australia | 0.938 |
| 4 | Luxembourg | 0.875 |
| 5 | Canada | 0.911 |
| 6 | Sweden | 0.916 |
| 7 | Switzerland | 0.913 |
| 8 | Ireland | 0.916 |
| 9 | Belgium | 0.897 |
| 10 | United States | 0.937 |
| 11 | Japan | 0.912 |
| 12 | Netherlands | 0.921 |
| 13 | Finland | 0.892 |
| 14 | Denmark | 0.901 |
| 15 | United Kingdom | 0.875 |
| 16 | France | 0.893 |
| 17 | Austria | 0.895 |

(The 2013/14 Human Development Report by the United Nations Development

HDI measures not only GDP, but also education, health services, literacy, communications, population characteristics, and so forth to obtain a broad assessment of a country's quality of life. Wealth in itself is not enough to assess a country's quality of life; instead, how wealth is used is a key factor in measuring the relative development of a country. In addition, it is necessary to examine a country's tax system and how it affects that country's development. The tax systems used in developed countries do not appear to have a negative effect on quality of life, but in spite of appearances, MBCS could improve life in developed countries faster than their current tax systems.

# CONCLUSION

The mutual benefit Bond system (MBCS) is based on incentive-based principles that prohibit interest and taxes. Interest and taxes have driven most of the world's population into poverty, and MBCS eliminates these two evils and offers the best hope for eliminating poverty in the shortest period of time. Most non-Muslim countries might consider MBCS a tool to spread Islam. As a result, they may be hesitant to implement MBCS; however, they will have no chance for survival if other countries implement it. The country that implements MBCS first will become an economic leader.

In order to raise enough money to meet national budgets, it is necessary to use a system of revenue collection that encourages people to participate in the scheme and produces large amounts of cash for a government quickly and at no extra cost or risk. The mutual benefit Bond/card system is an incentive-based revenue system that replaces current tax systems and encourages people to invest in their countries. MBCS is designed to:

1. Eliminate unfair financial burdens from all sectors of society;
2. Remove taxes, duties, and levies;
3. Revolutionize government revenue collection and liquidity;
4. Eliminate poverty;
5. Rebuild national infrastructures;
6. Restore law and order; and
7. Provide all citizens with equal opportunities.

MBCS is a very simple system. There are no checks and balances, hardly any documentation compared to the documentation in existing systems, and no chance of corruption. In addition, there is zero risk to existing government systems that generate revenue.

MBCS is easy to implement. It would be easy to find enough people willing to work for a MBCS agency, and all Bond vender positions would be filled in weeks. A country's treasury would print Bonds instead of bonds. A monetary agency could be set up in one week. As a result of the large amount of money Bonds vendors would make, it would take the monetary agency little time to establish its network, and this network would not cost the government any money. Given the benefits of MBCS, it would not be difficult to pass the legislation needed to implement the system.

No country can survive without implementing MBCS because this system will eliminate poverty, create massive employment, create an industrial revolution, improve law and order, eliminate drug-related problems and crimes, and eliminate the terrorism that is fueled by poverty. Any country that does not implement MBCS would face a public revolt and would be replaced by a government willing to implement this system.

A world without interest payments, poverty, and taxes, a world where law and order are the norm and a person has the opportunity to reach his or her potential on a level playing field would be a paradise to most people, but this paradise seems like a pipe dream, an illusion. It seems like an impossible dream to find a system that would eliminate interest payments and taxes and, at the same time, improve people's quality of life and enable them to reach their potential; however, using the mutual benefit Bond system, it is possible to create a world that is free of interest payments, poverty, and taxes. With MBCS, it is possible to create a paradise on Earth.

**FREQUENTLY ASKED**

**QUESTIONS**

**Note: India and its current economic situation are used as examples in these FAQs.**

**What is a MBCS Bonds?**

A MBCS Bonds can be viewed as a mandatory payment for goods and services. The bearer of these Bonds would be entitled to significant formularized discounts on the listed sale price/cost of goods and services if these Bonds are used with a cash payment. In the government sector, a consumer can pay in Bonds instead of cash, and the Bonds will be worth double the amount of currency. In the private sector, goods and services would be purchased with 15% in Bonds and the rest in cash.

### How can these Bonds be used? What are the benefits of using these Bonds?

These Bonds would be used to obtain reduced prices for goods and services offered by the government and the public sector. These Bonds will bring down the cost of living for a household consumer and reduce production costs for businesses.

### Who will sell MBCS Bonds, and who will be eligible to sell Bonds?

Unemployed and preferably educated people would be hired as MBCS agents. These people would have, at least, matriculated. They would be required to register with INMF for an annual fee of INR5, 000. INMF would conduct an intensive but short training course, and it would offer a 10% discount to agents and assigned them a monthly quota of Bonds worth INR300, 000, which would enable a bond agent to earn up to INR30, 000 a month.

### What if a person cannot pay the INR5, 000 registration fees?

If a person cannot pay the INR5, 000 registration fees, then his or her monthly quota will be reduced by 50% until the agent has paid the full registration fee.

### How do you control the artificially raised prices and subsidized prices of the commodities/services produced by private sector?

MBCS does not control the prices of the private sector; instead, it helps control prices by reducing the cost of production by at least 50% and eliminating taxes and import duties. Therefore, there is no artificial price or overprice in the private sector, and each product or service will be cheaper than the artificial price if the consumer uses 15% in Bonds and the rest in cash.

**Why pay for expenses that will be incurred in the future?**

Purchasing Bonds for future purchases will ensure that the consumer pays reduced prices because the Bonds are inexpensive and will buy products and services with reduced prices.

**Is there any financial incentive for this advance payment other than Bonds?**

No, there is no other financial incentive, and the consumer would get Bonds according to the prescribed sliding scale. However, consumers who buy Bonds during the discount period would receive more Bonds for their money and be entitled to waivers for import duties. In addition, they would be able to sell Bonds at a profit when the cost of Bonds increases later in a financial year.

**Does the purchase of INR100, 000 worth of Bonds entitle the consumer to any duty-free imports?**

A person or business that purchases Rs.100, 000 worth of bonds in the first month of a financial year is not entitled to any duty free option because he has purchased the bonds. In addition, 1,000 euro will exempt one million duties and this option will be available for first one month only and this option has to be used in one year but this duty free option can be sold partly or as a whole.

**How will the government control the under-invoicing of goods and services?**

People under-invoice in order to evade duties and taxes. There will be no need to under-invoice when custom duties are partially or completely waived.

**People who invest INR100, 000 receive extra Bonds, or they have the option to import goods and services duty free; however, people who invest less do not receive these benefits. Why?**

Incentives such as extra Bonds or a waiver of duties are available to people spending INR100, 000. Although some people cannot buy this many Bonds on their own, groups of low-income people can combine their funds and buy low-cost Bonds. Even if they cannot raise enough money to buy large amounts of Bonds, they will still receive a 30% to 60% reduction in their cost of living when they use their Bonds. In addition, a rich or clever businessperson can buy low-cost Bonds and negotiate a 4% to 8% discount from a bond agent. He or she would be able to sell these Bonds at the lowest rate to people who are unable to raise INR100, 000 and retain the discount as profit. This process can be repeated throughout the first month and result in high profits for the seller and low rates for the buyer.

**How can a government generate the same amount of revenue in subsequent years if Bonds are valid indefinitely and are in circulation right from the very first day?**

The use of Bonds is not restricted to individual consumers. Traders, manufacturers, importers, agriculturists, and corporate entities will also require Bonds for their day-to-day use. These bond users will buy and sell their merchandise through the India Monetary Fund (INMF). Spare Bonds can be sold on the open market at a profit or surrendered to the government to obtain duty-free options.

**The use of black money in this system will not generate the same amount of revenue in subsequent years. What remedies are available to the government?**

The government will invest black money or extra cash in high-tech companies, big business, and land reforms, and it will receive a profit from these investments every year. Therefore, the government will not have any need for black money after the first year.

## What is the organizational structure of INMF? How does it operate?

INMF will be a private organization selected by an open-bidding process. It will be responsible for selling Bonds through agents, collecting funds from agents, and depositing these funds in government accounts. INMF will operate regional offices, which will monitor branch offices in each city in their region. These branch offices will be linked by the latest information technology and will be located in the smallest village.

## How will INMF ensure transparent operations?

In order to ensure INMF's operations are transparent, the next three lowest bidders will be appointed auditors for a fixed fee. In addition, in the case of fraud or mistakes, these auditors will receive 50% of any penalties (i.e., 10 times the amount involved) imposed on INMF. The government will be the fourth auditor.

## Why will INMF need 100,000 offices with 50 to 100 million employees?

These offices and employees will be administrative in nature, which will ensure smooth, transparent operations, and they will be responsible for maintaining a record of bond sales. In addition, they will dispense Bonds to Bonds agents.

## How will INMF monitor sales and control revenue collection from bond agents?

Each agent will have a monthly quota of 300,000 Bonds. No agent can sell Bonds beyond his or her quota. This will ensure that each agent has the same opportunities, and each agent would be able to earn up to INR30, 000 a month.

**How would INMF eliminate or minimize the chances of bond agents committing fraud?**

All INMF records will be computerized, and a record for each agent will be maintained, which will reduce the chance of fraud or error. Any fraud or complaint against any agent will result in the termination of his or her services. The profits from fraud will be small, so most agents will not jeopardize their jobs for small payoffs.

**Currency is supported and backed by reserves. What supports or backs MBCS Bonds?**

Bonds do not need to be supported or backed by reserve currency because they can only be bought with actual currency, if a person does not have the money, his or she will not be able to purchase any Bonds.

**Who will print MBCS Bonds, and how will they be kept secure?**

The government will print MBCS bonds using the same infrastructure, standards, and security measures used to make present debt cards. Large amounts will be available as debit cards...

**What will be the size, color, and denominations of MBCS Bonds?**

MBCS bonds will be in the form of debit card. Their denominations will vary.

**What will it cost to print MBCS Bonds?**

Compared to the revenue generated by MBCS, the cost of making debit card is negligible and according to rough estimate each card holding unlimited amount of bonds will not cost more than 10 Rupees.

**The system looks very complicated and hardly possible to implement. Is this true?**

MBCS might seem complicated, but even people with limited education can understand it because it only involves two equations and is far simpler than the present tax system, which is only possible to understand with the help of tax consultants. In addition, the money system has been shifted from a binary system to the decimal system, which is considered difficult to understand and implement and used by very few people. Also, Bonds agents will educate people about the system.

**Will MBCS radically change India's taxation system?**

There will be no change in the tax structure (i.e., direct taxation) until and unless the government is able to meet it revenue needs using MBCS. Until that time, the tax system will remain intact. In addition, there will be no change in indirect taxation; however, MBCS Bonds will eventually be the only indirect taxation.

**Is there a time limit on the waiver in custom duty?**

The waiver of duty will be offered for a limited period of time. After a concessionary period, this waiver will not be available, and the person or business will be subject to the present duty structure. Category 3 businesses that sell their products through INMF will be able to import duty-free goods or services equal to the amount sold through INMF throughout the year.

**How will this system help alleviate poverty?**

This system will bring down the cost of living, and the necessities of life will be available for 30% to 60 % less than current market prices. In addition, this system will promote the creation of new industries and increased production in existing industries, which will increase the number of available jobs. This will definitely help reduce poverty in India. In a very first week, all unemployed people will be able to get job as a bond agent and earn a decent living at no cost to the government.

### How can a poor person obtain Bonds at the lowest rates?

Groups of low-income people can combine their funds and buy low-cost Bonds during the discount period. In addition, for a security deposit of INR100, a person can buy Bonds throughout the year for four or five Bonds per rupee.

### Will MBCS create real economic activity?

Yes. MBCS will produce an industrial boom because there will be no tax, no duty, and production costs will be reduced by 50%. This will create jobs and increase exports and reduce imports.

### How will MBCS affect industry in India?

India could be an economic giant if its socioeconomic constraints are removed. MBCS will remove these constraints and enable high-tech industries to grow. This growth in industries will reverse India's trade balance.

### What benefits or incentives are available to a person spending INR100, 000 to purchase Bonds in the first month of a financial year?

A person spending rs.100,000 or to purchase bonds in the first month of a financial year will be having following benefits: (1) If a person does not want bonds, he or she can receive a waiver of ten million Rupees on import duties for any legal imports, depending on the market rate of goods; (2) They can receive 600,000 bonds for routine bills throughout the year; (3) they can sell bonds for a profit at later stages once the concessionary period lapses; and (4) they can enter a draw for INR100 billion, which will be held daily.

### What is the life of Bonds? Do Bonds have a due date?

There is no due date, compulsory period of use or expiry date for MBCS Bonds. All Bonds will have an unlimited life and will continue in circulation in the same way currency circulates.

**What will the government do if the value of Bonds drops to INR0.1667?**

The Government of India will intervene and buy back Bonds at a cheaper price and raise the price of Bonds. This will not happen because Bonds can be surrendered for a duty-free option, provided 100,000 Bonds are surrendered.

**What effect will MBCS have on real estate?**

MBCS will likely crash the real estate market because the profit margin for Bonds will be much higher than the profit margin for property; therefore, it will be cheaper to build a house than buy one. It is estimated that it would could 50% less to build a house under MBCS.

**How will MBCS affect the stock market?**

Initially, MBCS will crash the stock market; however, it will recover and rise to new heights as a result of the elimination of taxes and a decrease in the price of government-controlled essential goods. Ultimately, the stock market will cease to exist because it is a form of gambling, and investing in Bonds carries almost no risk. In addition, this type of speculation or gambling is forbidden in Islam.

**Does implementing MBCS pose any risks to the government?**

MBCS is a unique, risk-free approach to revolutionizing the collection of government revenue. It does not require giving up current taxes until the system produces enough money to fund government activities. After that, MBCS will transform India into an open, transparent, free market where the government and citizens co-operate to drive prices down, create balanced budgets, and increase general investment. Therefore, there is absolutely no risk to the government.

**When will the government declare a tax-free holiday?**

Once the government has collected enough revenue, it will remove all taxes. This will further decrease prices. It is expected that the government will collect more than INR24 trillion in the first 2 hours of a financial year because of the incentives offered by MBCS, especially to people holding black money, which will be the main source of revenue collected in the first month.

**This system does not provide everyone with equal incentives. Why?**

The system is designed to provide financial incentives to everyone. Everyone will receive lower prices when using Bonds and cash to purchase goods and services.

**IMF puts many types of pressure on countries such as India. How will a country that implements MBCS deal with these pressures?**

At present, the government is forced to borrow short-, medium-, and long-term loans from IMF in order to finance cash imbalances, unplanned shortfalls in tax revenue, and infrastructure development. MBCS will create a positive cash flow for the government and lead to actual cash surpluses, which will eliminate the need to borrow money and make it possible to repay current loans.

**How will MBCS help establish interest free banking?**

The government must abandon all interest operations and use its cash surpluses from MBCS to promote investment through co-operation and partnership with the private sector. It would use surplus cash to establish and strengthen an Interest free financing system. The government would provide cash needed to finance this banking system.

**How will MBCS support interest free banking operations?**

The banks in India will offer MBCS bond accounts. The banks would have to establish special mandatory bond deposits. They would become as important a seller of Bonds as INMF. All investment in the private sector would be done through banks, with 80% of the cash provided by the government and 20% provided by the investor. The bank would be responsible for overseeing the business, and the government would provide all commodities and services below cost when the government is a partner in the business. The government would receive 40% of the profit, and 60% would be divided by the bank and investor. The state bank would oversee the whole lending process.

**People and organizations may hold more Bonds than required. Is not hoarding forbidden in the present system?**

In the present system, hoarding is not allowed because of its practical effects on the supply of critical items such as grain, water, and so forth. In MBCS, people would not be able to exercise monopolistic powers because Bonds would be freely available from INMF agents and private sellers. In addition, the central bank could intervene if banks try to manipulate bond rates. In this system, hoarding is not possible because Bonds would always be available from the government and the private sector.

**Will MBCS isolate India in international market? How will the government deal with imports and determine business relations with other countries under this system?**

MBCS is an internal system, and imports and business relationship with other countries will continue in the same way they do today. The only thing that will change is the waiver of duties under certain conditions, which has nothing to do with exporting countries.

**How does MBCS compensate the government for the loss of revenue from reduced prices for commodities and the waiver of duties?**

The sale of MBCS Bonds would more than compensate for the loss of revenue from reduced prices for commodities and the elimination of duties. In fact, the revenue generated by MBCS would many times the amount of money collected from the sale of commodities and duties.

**What is the benefit of Bonds to the general public?**

Bonds would reduce the price of every commodity or service provided by the government, and they would reduce the prices of goods and services provided by the private sector by 40% to 60%.

**How does this system support foreign exchange transactions?**

Under MBCS, any person remitting money from abroad through legitimate channels will receive 18 Bonds for each dollar. This rate would vary according to market conditions and would always be above the *Hawala* rate (at least 5%). This incentive would eliminate the need for the *Hawala* system. The government would sell surplus dollars to registered moneychangers at a slightly higher rate (19 Bonds per dollar). In this way, the public need for foreign exchange would be met without any difficulty.

**How does this system support foreign trade?**

As discussed above, MBCS reduces production and business costs by 50%. In such conditions, industrialists will have better opportunities for setting up new units or expanding/modernizing existing units. The low cost of manufacturing will make India's products very competitive on the international market. Very good quality products produced by hi-tech machinery and low prices will boost exports and domestic consumption, and consequently, imports would be reduced and India's trade balance would improve.

### Does this system benefit government employees?

MBCS would generate large amounts of money for the government, and as a result, the government would be able to improve its salary structure (i.e., increase salaries by at least three times present rates). This increase in salaries would improve the financial situation of employees, which, at present, makes them susceptible to corruption. Therefore, the level of corruption among government employees would decrease.

### What is the incentive for people with black money to participate in MBCS?

MBCS would enable people with black money to enter the legitimate economy and import goods duty free and sell these goods through INMF. This would double their profits and eliminate the risks associated with smuggling.

### How will MBCS help a business that does not deal with customers?

This type of business can pay a registration fee of INR100, 000 and buy Bonds every month at six Bonds per rupee. This business can get 600,000 Bonds for only INR100, 000. The higher the registration fee, the more cheap Bonds a business can purchase. The only condition is that the business must produce evidence of business operations and prove the registration fee has been paid. More than one business can pool their resources to take advantage of these cheap Bonds.

### How will MBCS help a business dealing with customers?

This type of business can pay a registration fee that is not less than INR10,000. They can buy twice the amount of Bonds collected from customers. For example, with a registration fee of INR10, 000, a business can collect up to 10,000 Bonds a month and buy 20,000 Bonds at a cost of INR3333, while collected Bonds will be replaced without any cost with new Bonds. The collection of Bonds will be according to the business' annual fee as shown in the bond table. With a registration fee of INR100,000, a business can collect 100,000 shares and buy three times the amount of collected shares at the rate of six Bonds per rupee. The higher the registration fee, the more Bonds a business can purchase at the cheapest rate. A shopkeeper would be eager to sell his or her merchandise for Bonds plus cash. The amount of Bonds accepted by a shopkeeper would depend on his or her needs. On the other hand, a customer would be more than happy to purchase merchandise with the help of Bonds because Bonds would reduce the price of merchandise because they have been purchased at a reduced rate.

**How will MBCS affect the cost of living?**

The cost of living will decrease as a result of the elimination of taxes, 50% decrease in the cost of goods and services, and pay raises.

**Will MBCS create inflation? Will people buy more goods and services than they need?**

MBCS will not create inflation because this system will result in a decrease in prices. It is true that with MBCS people will have more money to buy more goods and services, but that does not mean they will buy more than they need to improve their standard of living.

**If a business uses MBCS' duty free option to purchase a 40 lakh rupee car for 12 lakh rupees, what will prevent it from selling the car for 40 lakh rupees?**

When a business imports a 12 lakh rupee car using MBCS and tries to sell it for 40 lakh rupees, no one will buy it because they will be able to import the same car for 12 lakh rupees.

**How will MBCS help low-income people?**

Any person who uses government goods or services (e.g., travelling by railway) can use MBCS Bonds to obtain substantial discounts. For example, a railway ticket to Delhi may cost 400 rupees. In MBCS, the ticket may cost 800 Bonds. If the Bonds are purchased for six Bonds per rupee, then the ticket will cost two thirds less than the cost to purchase a ticket using rupees. With Bonds, a person will be able to save 40% to 70% on government-controlled goods and services, depending on the rate for Bonds.

**What is the cheapest price a person or business will be able to pay for MBCS Bonds?**

Bonds can be purchased for 16.67 paisa per bond, but this rate will only be available in the first month of a financial year or if the buyer has a special registration arrangement with INMF.

**It has been suggested that MBCS can operate at the same time as a current tax system. How will this work if people have to operate under existing tax laws?**

It would be necessary to enact legislation that safeguards the interests of a person using Bonds, and the government would not question a person's source of income.

**How will MBCS affect the fabric of our institutional makeup in terms of conceding power, authority, and so forth? How long would it take to be universally accepted and agreed?**

Authority tends to corrupt, and absolute authority corrupts absolutely. A large amount of time would have to be devoted to not antagonizing people in power. This is why INMF would be an autonomous institution. As soon as India becomes economically self-sufficient and debt free, MBCS would spread like wild fire.

**It seems unrealistic to predict that MBCS will solve India's revenue problems in 30 days. Is it not true that a project of this magnitude can easily take a few years to implement?**

It can take several years to implement a system such as MBCS. In order to ensure a smooth transition from the current tax system to MBCS, INMF will operate as an independent system that operates parallel to the current tax system. Once MBCS shows that it can work, the current tax system will become redundant.

**Can Bonds be stolen?**

Yes. The possibility of theft exists for any type of currency or bond.

**No marketing and advertising expenses have been mentioned during the discussion about MBCS. Why?**

The one million bond agents would educate the public about the benefits of using MBCS Bonds. In addition, INMF would need to educate the public using some television and radio commercials.

www.ingramcontent.com/pod-product-compliance
Lightning Source LLC
Chambersburg PA
CBHW030902180526
45163CB00004B/1670